Property of Title IV

Student Voice

Student Voice

From Invisible to Invaluable

Michael Lubelfeld,
Nick Polyak, and
PJ Caposey

AASA COPUBLISHING ROWMAN & LITTLEFIELD
Lanham · Boulder · New York · London

Published in partnership with the American Association of School Administrators

Published by Rowman & Littlefield
A wholly owned subsidiary of The Rowman & Littlefield Publishing Group, Inc.
4501 Forbes Boulevard, Suite 200, Lanham, Maryland 20706
www.rowman.com

Unit A, Whitacre Mews, 26–34 Stannary Street, London SE11 4AB

British Library Cataloguing in Publication Information Available

Library of Congress Cataloging-in-Publication Data Available

ISBN: 978-1-4758-4001-8 (cloth : alk. paper)
ISBN: 978-1-4758-4002-5 (pbk. : alk. paper)
ISBN: 978-1-4758-4003-2 (electronic)

∞™ The paper used in this publication meets the minimum requirements of American National Standard for Information Sciences—Permanence of Paper for Printed Library Materials, ANSI/NISO Z39.48–1992.

Printed in the United States of America

Contents

List of Figures and Tables

LIST OF FIGURES

LIST OF TABLES

Foreword

Dear colleagues,

Student Voice: From Invisible to Invaluable offers far more than current educational research and perspective on the power of learners to fully participate in the leadership of our schools and in their own learning. This book takes readers seeking solutions to challenges faced by today's educators into a deep learning experience beyond the normative culture of contemporary schools. Authors Mike, Nick, and PJ courageously speak to the importance of democratic schools as spaces in which learners are encouraged to inform and shape the work of educators to fully support students individually or as communities of learners.

Democratic spaces for learners are not created by chance. In fact, as you delve into this book, you will find that educators who value the voices of all young people believe engaging youth in a structured feedback cycle is critical to the process of evaluating educators' success in meeting the needs of learners of all ages.

As the authors note, when students spend 170 days or more in school, they become experts in effective teaching. They know good teaching when they experience it. They understand the importance of positive relationships with adults. And young people, based on youth survey data, clamor for the opportunity to share their feedback with educators who have ultimate control over their learning lives.

The authors also advance a compelling argument why schools must transform rather than just sustain the traditional hierarchies of an archaic 20th-century education model that still defines most districts, schools, and classrooms. They illustrate why change must occur and use numerous concrete examples to illustrate how a school's culture can evolve and become responsive to learners when student voices are elevated.

Their narrative speaks to the significant positive changes that occur when hierarchies are flattened and playing fields leveled as a result of adults actively eliciting students to share their perspectives and become a part of the solutions that adults seek to better serve all learners.

As you read through the book, the ASK'EM acronym developed by PJ, Nick, and Mike offers a valuable tool to organize and apply what these authors have learned in their boots on the groundwork to elevate student voices in any situation in a school setting. It's simple, is easy to recall, and gets to the heart of strategy to engage learners in adult decision-making processes. The authors say just ask kids and they will respond.

After you ask, then offer your Support, Know the feedback and your research, Empower their leadership and participation, and Monitor that adults follow through on actions along with assessment of the results. As you move through this book, the ASK'EM frame will help you consider how to customize your own strategies for engaging students to lead with you.

How important is it for educators to give students the chance to provide feedback to their teachers? The authors provide their own action research, but they also point to John Hattie's meta-analysis research as a rationale for making student feedback to teachers an essential part of professional learning for educators.

Hattie's research identifies feedback as a strategy under educators' control that has one of the highest effect sizes of the 195 strategies he has evaluated. As Nick, PJ, and Mike note, student feedback to teachers represents a linchpin engagement strategy, indeed, one of the most powerful ways that teachers can positively impact student learning.

Amplifying student voice by actively engaging students in feedback to teachers is quite important if a school district is serious about closing gaps in achievement. However, feedback is just one strategy among many that intentionally increase opportunities for student voices to become strong in schools. In *Student Voice: From Invisible to Invaluable*, students and educators share personal stories of how the voices of young people can influence the work of a learning organization.

I especially appreciated the examples of how teens have helped shape and form digital learning tool uses and also problem solved with educators to discover how to best support students' responsible use of technology. Not only do the authors describe actions they have taken in response to digital learning insights they have gained from students, such as unblocking Twitter, but they also describe students as active leaders and partners with educators in the decision-making processes regarding digital citizenship curricula and effective uses of 1:1 technologies.

Students see technology applications differently, and those have become a second language, indeed a digital language, for learners. In today's world, educators must integrate technology applications across curricula and also attend to and even supervise how children learn to play in the virtual "playground" of the Internet. Adults would never abdicate their roles as coaches and teachers who enter playgrounds with their toddlers or kindergartners as they learn to safely use slides, monkey bars, and swings.

Why, then, would we stand outside the virtual world "playground" and simply hope our young people safely learn to negotiate communication, entertainment, and learning opportunities in that world? This book offers you concrete and useful examples of how to solicit students' perspectives, their helpful leadership, and their ideas to better engage students in digital learning.

Incorporating student voices into their narrative, the authors use those to illustrate what can grow from student empowerment. It's apparent from reading those voices that when we ask learners for input, we must be ready for them to go much farther than we would have ever anticipated. Kyla G.'s story in chapter 3, in her own voice, lays out how once she became engaged, her voice powered up well beyond what the adults supporting her might have anticipated.

The phrase "invisible to invaluable" captures the amplification of her voice as she shifted from being a participant in a cyber-security event to actively leading her own events and activities in her school, then influencing her local community, and ultimately developing her own programs and communication network to influence adults and students alike in Illinois and across the nation. Her work was fueled by her passion, marrying an interest in digital learning, cyber-security, and community outreach.

We must be ready, as the work in this book shows, for amplification of students' voices to create a high degree of agency by design, and, ultimately, for students to see how their voices can influence changes for the good in their schools and communities. You will find example after example that illustrates when students realize their voices have power, they begin to see themselves as authentic leaders who have important points of view to offer.

Rather than being the subjects of educational research, in the school districts featured in this book, students have become members of research and development teams. They have helped staff with a continuum of decisions from determining what digital tools will be purchased for them to use to how to build communication campaigns to reach parents and students.

Incorporating student voices adds time to the decision-making process—if you plan to use student feedback in authentic ways. As the authors point out, authentic elevation of student voices isn't an add-on at the last minute to say you received student feedback or student assistance only sought when a problem becomes thorny in a community. When adults value that students routinely think with them in a classroom, a school, or a district, the young people come to the table with all their diverse thinking and get to experience how their perspectives are meaningful.

Creating democratic spaces in schools to privilege all student voices also leads to authentic inclusivity of students in a variety of activities. This means making arrangements with parents to support younger children to be a part of the process. It may mean including teens in activities that traditionally are reserved for adults, such as site visits to other schools.

It certainly, as the authors note, means that you may hear feedback you don't want to hear from students, feedback that can take you in a direction that adults in the room didn't anticipate. You have to be ready for that because as stated in one of my favorite quotes (chapter 4 in the book):

> Students have had education done to them for many years. Let's do education with them. When technology, or anything new, is introduced into the learning environment, we implore you: don't assume the kids want or understand the changes.

Whether you choose to read this book in one sitting or in chunks, each chapter offers a clear pathway to help you navigate your way to finding student voices in your own learning community and creating situations that support these learners to join the discussion about their own schooling. In environments where student perspectives are valued, adults get as close as possible to knowing the learning needs of students. When young people discover that adults really mean it when they ask for their ideas, suggestions, points of view, and assistance, they become active leaders and participants.

Organizations that embrace student voices change the game when it comes to using a Plan-Do-Study-Act model and making students a part of strategic solutions to the grand challenges faced by schools everywhere. Young people will hold adults accountable to that process and to seeing beyond that which adults do best, to plan and study. Young people by their very nature do and act. They come to school every day prepared to do the work put in front of them. They have opinions about that work.

They have perspectives on how they learn best. They know, as student Charlie Zielinski (chapter 8) discovered in his high school, that it's the adults who set the tone for a school's social and cultural responsiveness to learner differences. Fortunately, he landed in a high school where the adults had learned to value student voices representing differences and to set a tone of equity in how students found support from adults. The adults had not just studied the problems of equity, regardless of the source, but had taken actions to actively address equity issues. As Charlie says in the book:

> I always thought it was the students that helped make an environment like that, but as high school went by, I realized that it was the staff and the administration that made that environment. They were truly committed to make every student feel accepted.

Equity is, in the opinion of many educators including me, the grand challenge that schools have faced for generations and perhaps even more expansive a challenge today than in any other time in the history of American education.

We no longer can settle for communities of "haves and have-nots" in schools if we are committed to an "all means all" learning philosophy. We adults can't espouse inclusivity by letting all the kids into our educational dance and then be okay with many of them standing around the walls never being invited to actually dance.

Educators create the culture of our schools. We control who gets equity of access to quality teaching and learning. We are solution-finders to the problems that educators face. In this book, the authors identify some of those problems and with clarity describe how they as leaders have looked to the full range of potential in their communities, most importantly, bringing students together with adults to generate solutions and then act to implement those solutions. As a result, they've empowered student leaders across a range of demographics.

They've heard student input that has helped them avoid blind spots. They've supported learners to acquire success skills for life, not just to pass academic tests. They realize the need for a new generation of leaders, social activists, entrepreneurial thinkers, community volunteers, political voices and policy makers, and simply great employees, employers, family members, and citizens. Student voices matter because one day they will become adult voices that matter.

Who wouldn't want that for learners everywhere? Don't read just a few pages of *Student Voice: From Invisible to Invaluable* and let work get in the way of finishing it. Read it. Then go implement your own ASK'EM strategies as you implement Plan-Do-Study-Act goals. Your goals can become reality with the help of student voices in your own classroom, school, or district.

Thank you to PJ, Nick, and Mike for taking the time to share your work with all of us.

Regards,
Pam Moran
Superintendent

Preface

Student Voice: From Invisible to Invaluable is about why today's leaders need to connect with students and how to accomplish true success by giving students a voice in their own education. The premise of this book is that student voice is often, for some inconceivable reason, invisible.

The failure to systematically include students and listen to their viewpoints is a contributing factor, which explains why schools have changed little since the 19th century. This book will explore many topics ranging from digital citizenship to teacher evaluation, and we sincerely believe that by leveraging the voice of students as collaborative leaders, true school and educational transformation can and will occur.

The book is based around two central questions:

- Why should today's school leaders engage student voice from a leadership perspective as collaborators in leading?
- How can today's school leaders engage student voice from a leadership perspective as collaborators in leading?

The core beliefs that drive this book are largely based on research. These beliefs include the idea that the single most impactful person in a student's learning journey is the teacher. The second most impactful is the principal (Marzano & Waters, 2005). If the teacher is a manager and the principal is a leader, congruence in the approaches of engaging the student in his own learning must exist. Additionally, confidence is necessary to amplify student voice in our schools. One of the five exemplary practices of leadership (Kouzes & Posner, 2007) is enable others to act.

Enabling Others to Act is the behavior of a confident leader. Leaders who understand the strengths of their employees and their potential for more responsibility feel confident in **enabling others** to take control and initiative. **Enabling** is a leadership behavior while controlling and directing is a management behavior. (Retrieved from http://www.business-leadership-qualities.com/leadershipbehavior-3.html)

We submit that taking student voice from invisible to invaluable reflects the choices made by confident leaders. Leaders in the classroom (teachers), leaders in the office (principals), and leaders in the central office (superintendents) must exist at all levels to truly listen to student voice and for school evolution and even transformation to be possible. Throughout this book, we will continually work to convince the reader of why this paradigm shift leading to an increase in student voice is necessary and give tips and techniques on how to get the work done.

Our leadership journeys allow us to test theories of leadership and put into practice beliefs, hypotheses, thoughts, and actions. While we lead with other adults and members of the typical school community—teachers, board members, administrators, and parents—we have engaged students in leadership as well. We share our successful leadership experiences and examples of making student voices invaluable in actual leadership and governance.

Through deliberate elevation and partnership with our main clients and customers (students), we have proven that a truly collaborative and engaged process is possible, plausible, preferred, and practical. Student voice is a topic we will help employ to move collaboration with students from superficial to significant. In *Student Voice: From Invisible to Invaluable*, we identify several ways student voice can be meaningfully amplified to create a new reality of schooling and leadership.

This transformation is truly a win-win for students and leaders. Educators must simply do two things to begin the paradigm shift necessary to take this forward. The first is easy—believe in the brilliance of your students. The second is hard—relinquish some element of control. This book will help walk the reader through both of these steps while focusing on precise areas of potential change within your classroom, school, or district.

Through problem analysis and actionable examples, the reader can replicate meaningful and impactful student voice and engagement in their systems tomorrow. The examples in this book will elevate student voice from invisible to invaluable. As "practitioner-scientists," we provide examples from the field to share how valuable and impactful student voice is and can become in any system when leveraged appropriately.

EDUCATIONAL CONTEXT—WHY THIS BOOK IS NECESSARY

Around the nation, many leaders are implementing various forms of personalized learning. The synergy between student learning and growth and teacher direction and knowledge grows exponentially when student voice is real, true, and authentic. Long gone are the days where compliance ruled the priorities of teachers and schools. We will examine personalized learning and how student voice can be amplified through personalized learning environments in chapter 7.

We are encouraged by groups like Education Reimagined, who "see the current school-centered education system transformed into one that's truly learner-centered. It is a future with thriving learners surrounded by engaged and dedicated educators, parents, and communities. [They] offer [their] vision as a beacon for all those dedicated to transforming education in America" (retrieved from https://education-reimagined.org). The Education Reimagined "North Star" as shown in figure 0.1 provides an overview framework of what learner-centered school organization contains.

This North Star grouping is aligned with our experiences, observations, research, and practice as it relates to transforming educational systems from the current 19th-century teacher/adult-centered ones to the 21st and 22nd centuries and beyond. Our vision is for student/learner-centered systems that we're compelled to create. As Mike and Nick wrote in *The Unlearning Leader: Leading for Tomorrow's Schools Today* (2017 Rowman & Little-field), we all must unlearn so that we can learn and relearn—change is not an optional process.

The reader of this book will see the North Star concepts of the Education Reimagined vision woven throughout the tapestry of the book. Today's leaders, teachers, students, and pretty much all constituent stakeholder groups must embody the 4Cs: communication, collaboration, critical thinking, and creativity. Teaching students what it means to "be at the table" and teaching students how to think "outside of the box" open up pathways never before seen or applied in modern school systems.

These pathways can be replicated and refined with student leadership experiences in "real life" through their schooling experiences. Student voice does not "just happen"; the success of this fundamental shift in how we "do school" is dependent upon shared vision, deliberate engagement, and by teaching students how to be a part of the process. We share examples of how

COMPETENCY-BASED

PERSONALIZED, RELEVANT & CONTEXTUALIZED

LEARNER AGENCY

SOCIALLY EMBEDDED

OPEN-WALLED

Figure 0.1 Education Reimagined Concepts

and why the future belongs to the students and that the present-day leaders can do much to set them up for success.

With this type of engaged and partner leadership, we will allow future generations to bear witness to transformed systems of schooling and society. Long gone are the days of "sage on the stage" in order to support the "guide on the side." Leaders can engage students and establish new norms so their input becomes invaluable. This is a call to action book for all people interested in transforming education and to improving the world.

The learning purposes and unique features of this book include:

- Establish, propose, and reinforce the "how" and the "why" for including student voice in leadership decision making
- Provide leaders with actionable case studies and examples from the field for implementation
- Model and share new ways of incorporating authentic student voice
- Reflection questions that will generate thought and conversation around each chapter
- End of chapter feature ASK'EM, an actionable acronym, to both reinforce chapter concepts and examples as well as a call to action: Ask, Support, Know, Empower, Monitor
- Stop-Think-Act prompts, questions, and problems of practice
- Commentaries and essays from students and educational leaders throughout the book. This provides additional voices on the topics on progressing with student voice from invisible to invaluable

Acknowledgments

We would like to thank Tom Koerner, Jimmy Minichello, Carlie Wall, and everyone else at Rowman & Littlefield and the AASA for their support, guidance, and encouragement.

We would also like to thank the incredible students, teachers, and community members with whom we have worked, currently work with, and those with whom we will work in the future. Finally, we wish to thank the innovative and creative folks at Education Reimagined for offering guidance for our future work.

Mike: I want to thank my supportive and wonderful wife, Stephanie, and my incredible children, Maya and Justin, for supporting the writing process. I want to thank my good friend, Jeff Zoul, for inspiration, encouragement, advice, and modeling the way for many years and with many laughs and successes. I want to thank the many students who have, and who continue to, engaged, inspired, and empowered me to lead, learn, and grow. I want to thank the members of the Deerfield Public Schools District 109 Board of Education for supporting my continued personal professional growth. I want to thank Brad, Dennison, Jared, and the HUMANeX Ventures teams for allowing my voice to impact research, practice, and growth. Finally, I want to thank Nick and PJ for a great partnership and collaborative book-writing experience. I'm looking forward to continued leadership adventures together.

Nick: I would like to thank our outstanding Leyden students, staff, administration, and Board of Education for teaching me about the value of student voice. I want to thank my wife, Kate, and our children, Chase, John, Ben, and Gabe, for supporting all of dad's crazy projects. I want to thank our parents and community members who trust us to Educate, Enrich, and Empower their children every day at our schools.

PJ: 2017 has been an incredible year, but a difficult one. In order to be able to continue to pursue my passions and dreams, others have to sacrifice. This is not lost on me. Sincere appreciation and thanks to my family (Jacquie, Jameson, Jackson, Caroline, and Anthony) who far too often get the short end of the stick. Additionally, thank you to my faculty, staff, administration, and Board of Education for your trust in me and support in all aspects of my professional growth. Lastly, thank you to the two coauthors. I am extremely excited about this book, but your friendship and collegiality mean more to me than this book ever could.

Introduction

We wrote this book to help elevate the power and influence of student voice in the transformation and leadership of our schools. Before we get into the details of our book, we thought it would be helpful to review some historical information about the public schools in the United States in general.

This context helps frame where we have been, where we are, and where we propose we go in school leadership. Recently the conversation about why education is still stuck in the 19th-century structures has permeated discussion across the nation. We are sharing a call to action that will propel us into the future with learners and student voice at the center of leadership, planning, and transformation!

USA Public School History 1647–1785 (retrieved from http://www.arc. org/content/view/100/217/).

1647

The General Court of the Massachusetts Bay Colony decrees that every town of fifty families should have an elementary school and that every town of 100 families should have a Latin school. The goal is to ensure that Puritan children learn to read the Bible and receive basic information about their Calvinist religion.

1785

The Continental Congress (before the U.S. Constitution was ratified) passes a law calling for a survey of the "Northwest Territory" which included what was to become the state of Ohio. The law created "townships," reserving a portion of each township for a local school. From these "land grants" eventually came the U.S. system of "land grant universities," the state public universities that exist today. Of course, in order to create these townships, the Continental Congress assumes it has the right to give away or sell land that is already occupied by Native people.

Upon becoming the secretary of education in Massachusetts in 1837, Horace Mann (1796–1859) worked to create a statewide system of professional teachers, based on the Prussian model of "common schools," which referred to the belief that everyone was entitled to the same content in education. Mann's early efforts focused primarily on elementary education and on preparing teachers.

John Adams insisted on the necessity of "education for every class and rank of people down to the lowest and the poorest" in order to make sure that the nation would we well governed and united." (Nevins 135).

Township government is still in place in 2017, and the "land grants" help explain how and why school district boundaries go in and out of municipal boundaries (they predate them in many instances).

It's also interesting (or shocking) to note that Horace Mann's Prussian inspired system of age/grade organization in schools still exists in the United States. Since 1848, we in education have accepted the concept that all children with the same age are best suited together for all learning experiences in school. One hundred sixty-nine years later, in 2017, we ask: Is this system relevant in today's information age?

Why has it been in place for more than a century and a half? The one-room-schoolhouse method of organization appears to have endured for nearly two centuries. Do we have to wait until the Prussian model is also two centuries old prior to changing?

In *Student Voice: From Invisible to Invaluable*, we challenge the notion that the public-school system in the United States should still be based upon antiquated, mid-19th-century Prussian values. Where is Prussia today? (Don't answer that—it was rhetorical.) We contend that the next iteration of schools and schooling must reflect the input and voice of the students for maximizing success, growth, and evolution. Nearly two centuries into the age-based system, it's time to rethink our structures and worldview.

The recently published works of John Hattie (1999–2017) as well as the widely published "effect sizes" of instructional practices (retrieved from https://visible-learning.org/hattie-ranking-influences-effect-sizes-learning-achievement/) suggest that instructional practices yielding an effect size of 0.4 equal about a typical year's growth for a typical student. Recently there were newly found concepts that yield up to a 1.62 effect size (or, conceptually four years' worth of growth in one year).

There were some new and some old favourites at the top of the list. Six of these had such a strong effect that they would distort any attempt to graph them. I call these super factors. Including them in the graph would distort the important differences between the other 188 factors. So I have listed them here.

The 6 super factors were:

1. Teacher estimates of achievement ($d = 1.62$). . . . this reflects the accuracy of teachers' knowledge of students in their classes.
2. Collective teacher efficacy ($d = 1.57$). This . . . involves helping all teachers on the staff to understand that the way they go about their work has a significant impact on student results . . . it involves stopping them from using other factors (e.g. home life, socio-economic status, motivation) as an excuse for poor progress.
3. Self-reported grades ($d = 1.33$). . . . this is a factor that teachers can't use to boost student achievement. It simply reflects the fact that students are pretty good at knowing what grade they will get on their report card before they read it.
4. Piagetian levels ($d = 1.28$). . . . it simply means that students who were assessed as being at a higher Piagetian level than other students do better at school. . .
5. Conceptual change programs ($d = 1.16$). This is a promising one. . . . Conceptual change textbooks introduce concepts and at the same time discuss relevant and common misconceptions. While the current research is limited to science textbooks in secondary school, it is reasonable to predict that when teachers apply this same idea to introduce any new concept in their classroom, it could have a similar impact.
6. Response to Intervention ($d = 1.07$). This is a structured program designed to help at-risk students make enough progress and ideally achieve comparable results to their peers. (Retrieved from http://www.evidencebased teaching.org.au/hattie-effect-size-2016-update/).

These six highly impactful concepts and practices relate to learning about students in one's classroom. Sounds simple, but to truly know what your students need to learn, how they learn, and what they have learned that is wrong and needs to be unlearned, all of these together incorporate a recipe for huge success and growth beyond the arbitrary "one year's growth." Who is to say what "every child" should learn in one year.

We submit that these precepts about schooling are preposterous and harmful. The practices handed down from our Prussian friends to Horace Mann, the practices that once served us well, may very well be destroying our modern school system and thus our future society. Let's stop limiting learning and growth. Let's stop stifling creativity. Let's reengage our students and increase their excitement and energy as they progress through their education. Let's reverse the current trends of disengagement as children become educated. Let's make student voice invaluable instead of invisible. Let's reverse the trends shown in figure 0.2.

Looking to visions like the Education Reimagined transformational vision for education in the United States, we frame our work in both concept and practice. After reading *Student Voice: From Invisible to Invaluable*, the reader will know why and how the move to learner-centered, student-involved leadership is not only necessary but also inevitable for our society to grow and prepare for the future.

We are organizing this book into four parts with nine total chapters. The book is about incorporating student voice, student input, and student presence into decision making and school improvement planning. This book requires philosophical or paradigm change and behavioral change from the adults in our schools in order to ensure success.

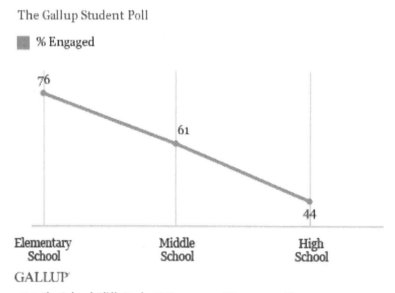

Figure 0.2 The School Cliff: Student's Engagement Drops over Time

We take the surface-level student involvement often seen and share actionable steps leaders can take immediately to incorporate deep and meaningful student voice in leadership.

In part I: Student Voice in Governance, Service, and Character Education, we share chapters 1 and 2: chapter 1: Decision Making—Classroom to Boardroom; chapter 2: Building Our Community of Learners: Leverage Our Primary Conduit to Our Communities. Throughout the book, we weave in student commentaries as well as practitioner commentaries.

In part II: Student Voice in Technology Instruction, we address digital citizenship in chapter 3: From Digital Natives to Digital Citizens as well as impact of 1:1 learning on students in chapter 4: Student Learning through 1:1 Initiatives.

In part III: Student Voice in Design and Communication, we consider student voice in school design and district communications. In this part, we have chapter 5: School Design/Structures: What Is School? and chapter 6: Student Voice in District Communication—PR Branding. In addition, in this part of the book, we address student voice in learning design in chapter 7: Personalized Learning.

We close the book with part IV: Student Voice in Equity and Evaluation with chapter 8: Helping Students Define Equity: Engage Students in the Equity Discussion and chapter 9: Teacher Evaluation: Give Students a Voice.

After reading this book, the reader will have a multitude of actionable ideas, experiences, examples, and suggestions for elevating student voice in their organizations. Every chapter has the unique ASK'EM feature, which cements the main premise that if we just "ask 'em" we can elevate student voice from invisible to invaluable. From digital citizenship to design and furniture, we share the why and how of empowering student voice as partners in leadership.

Part I

STUDENT VOICE IN GOVERNANCE, SERVICE, AND CHARACTER EDUCATION

Chapter 1

Decision Making—
Classroom to Boardroom

Government of the people, by the people, for the people shall not perish
from the Earth.

—Abraham Lincoln

Allow Students In on the Big Decisions
Students on the School Board
Example from the Field
What Do Students Think about Character Education?
Summary
Guest Commentary from Recent Graduate Michael Motyka
Guest Commentary from Student School Board Member Noelle Lowther

Reflection Questions

How do you engage stakeholders in the decision-making process?
In what ways can you increase student voice/student agency at the board
level?
Do you measure how often students are engaged at the board level in presentations or initiative planning?

Stop-Think-Act

Stop: Do you have students on committees as honorary members or as "real"
members?
Think: In what ways can you elevate student voice on governance and opera-
tional decisions?
Act: Ask students if they want to be decision makers and if so, in what areas?

ALLOW STUDENTS IN ON THE BIG DECISIONS

Schools often allow students to participate in superfluous and nonessential decision-making activities. In this chapter, we explore having the courage to engage students in true and meaningful decision making from the classroom all the way to the boardroom. An emphasis is put on sharing ways that student input can be equalized with adult voice as changes are made in schools.

Student voice doesn't need to stop at the classroom level or the building level. If you are to truly commit to the importance of student voice, it needs to be infused at all levels of the organization, including the school board.

According to the Center for Public Education,

> The local school board is a critical public link to public schools. Whether elected or appointed, school board members serve their communities in several important ways. First and foremost school boards look out for students. Education is not a line item on the school board's agenda—it is the only item.

Before discussing the role of student voice in the boardroom, it's important to define the role and responsibilities of a school board. The selection process of school board members varies by state. In some areas, they are elected, and in others, they are appointed. In some areas, board members need to represent different geographic areas, and in others, the selection is open to all residents of the district's boundaries.

Some boards are comprised of three or five members; others have seven, or nine, or more. Some board members are paid and have offices in the school districts, while most serve as volunteers in addition to their personal careers. School boards are not meant to get into the details and the management of a school district. By design, they hire four distinct As (the chief Administrator, an Auditor, the district's Attorney, and an Architect).

The architect needs to make sure that the buildings are safe and kept up to all codes and safety standards. The attorney guides the board in all matters dealing with law, statutes, and interpretation of school code. The auditor provides an unbiased set of eyes on the district's finances to make sure that the public's resources are being used responsibly. Finally, the board hires the chief administrator, or the superintendent, who is responsible for managing and leading the district.

No matter the size of the board or the manner of selection, school board members are meant to serve their local constituencies. Much like the electoral college system was designed to represent the intentions of each state, each school board member is meant to represent the collective will of the local community or at least their part of the local community. School districts suffer when board members do not understand the nature of this responsibility. When individuals bring their own priorities or agendas to the boardroom, the system can cease to function as it is designed.

Each board member is able to bring the perspectives of his or her neighbors, local parents, and the business community. The "end users" of schools are the students, and they are often overlooked as a constituency of the school district. When you include students on the school board, you acknowledge the importance of their constituency and you take advantage of their unique perspectives when it comes to district governance.

STUDENTS ON THE SCHOOL BOARD

Whether spoken or unspoken, the inclusion of students on the school board sends a message to your community. It says that you value the input and perspective that only students can provide. It says that your organization is not arbitrarily hierarchical in nature. It says that your adult board members seek to be connected with every level of the organization. It tells your students that this school system is for them and it wants to best meet their needs, now and in the future. There are a variety of ways to choose student board members; in some districts, an election is held among the student body. Students can be asked to apply for the opportunity based on preset standards or requirements. A district can utilize existing student leaders via student council members, class presidents, and others. Really, the selection process can be whatever makes sense locally, as long as the end result is bringing student voice to the district's governance and decision-making process.

A frequent question about student board members is, "What can they do and what can't they do when it comes to board business." A common approach is that the students can do everything except cast votes and participate in closed-session discussion due to the sensitive nature of some of the topics. That means that the student board members would receive the same communications, participate in discussions, and provide input on all topics and conversations. They should be allowed to attend regional school board events, state conferences, and whatever other events make sense and will help them best perform their roles along with the adults in the boardroom.

A word of caution: If your district names student board members on an honorary basis, you need to ask whether or not you are actually getting the voice of students. In order to benefit from the knowledge and expertise of your students, the full board needs to actually listen to and, when appropriate, act upon the recommendations from their students. Not every thought or idea from a student board member deserves action, just like not every idea from a single adult member deserves action. However, the students should have equal opportunities to make their points heard.

In addition to participation in regular debates and discussions, another suggestion is to add a standing agenda item for student board member reports. This simple practice gives them a regular opportunity to share concerns brought to them from their classmates. It also allows those students to develop their leadership skills and comfort with public speaking.

In schools, we talk about the importance of teaching our students the 21st-century skills of creativity, collaboration, communication, and critical thinking. This scenario allows student board member to communicate and collaborate with the adult members. Together they can use critical thinking skills to find creative solutions to problems in the district. Using student voice in this way allows those students to not only live out those 21st-century skills but also learn about the importance of civic engagement in their local communities.

EXAMPLE FROM THE FIELD

At Leyden Community High School District 212 in Franklin Park, Illinois, the Board of Education is comprised of seven elected members. In 2016, they decided to add two student board members, one from each of the district's high schools. Vanessa Gallegos was selected to represent East Leyden High School, and Noelle Lowther was selected to represent West Leyden High School.

At that time, the average tenure of each board member was over twelve years, meaning that this group had been leading the school district together for a long time. In August 2016, those two students took the oath of office and began their year of service on the board. A commentary and reflection on that experience is included at the end of this chapter. In figure 1.1, we show the Leyden Board with student members.

Several months into the year, the board was debating how to handle a particular topic. One of the board members, Jim Lima, paused and turned toward the student members. He did something very simple; he asked them what they thought. After both of them provided their input and their thoughts on the impact for students, a great moment occurred. Board member Jack Tobin looked up and down the board table and said, "Why haven't we been doing this forever?"

That Board of Education operates by a very simple motto on the wall of the boardroom. In large letters, that motto reads, "What's Best for the Kids." As often as they have referred to that motto over the years, it wasn't until that board meeting that they felt the power of including student voice in helping them put that motto into action.

Figure 1.1   Leyden Board with Student Members (Retrieved from: http://www.leyden212. org/domain/10)

Over the course of that first year, the student board members participated in regular discussions while also bringing up concerns and ideas from their classmates. They brought up the fact that the public-address system was hard to hear at football games and echoed student desires for an artificial turf field and a lacrosse team. They pointed out that some calendar events conflicted with several sports' senior nights, which would impact attendance and opportunities to participate.

When their service came to an end in May 2017, the board meeting became one of the most memorable in the district's history. Both student board members had an opportunity to share about their experience. They shed tears being sad to see their time come to an end. However, their parents, their adult colleagues on the board, and others in attendance were also seen wiping away tears. What started out as seeking student voice on the board developed into relationships, trust, and a partnership benefiting the district and all of the people involved.

WHAT DO STUDENTS THINK ABOUT CHARACTER EDUCATION?

When it comes to student voice, educators have a dual purpose. First, we need to recognize our students as our ultimate end users and incorporate their voice into the educational system we provide for them. Second, we need to acknowledge that students are works in progress. We have a responsibility to provide them with the opportunities and experiences that will help them develop their voice, their understanding of the world, and their place within it.

Every student grows up in a particular community. They know their families, their friends and communities, and their schools. In their schools, they are taught about the world, but few have a chance to actually experience the world. Worse than that, students who grow up in poverty have significantly fewer opportunities to see and experience the world beyond where they have lived and grown up.

That reality drove an interesting conversation at Leyden High School District 212 in Illinois in 2016. For several years, the district provided a global service learning trip to Mexico where students had the opportunity to volunteer at an orphanage and a rural school. They had a chance to see the realities of the world and personally make a difference in the lives of others.

Dr. Polyak and the school board discussed this opportunity and the cost of this trip. While it was an amazing opportunity for students, over 50 percent of Leyden's students are classified as "low-income." If a school district provides opportunities like this, but over half of the district can never afford to participate, do they really have an opportunity, or not?

With that question in mind, the school district deliberately decided to do two things. They expanded the district's global service learning opportunities to include both the annual trip to Mexico and an additional trip to serve in rural Peru.

Then the board vowed to fund those trips down to the last $500 per student. While this didn't make global service learning available to all students in the district, it did make it accessible to all students. The board acknowledged their responsibility to help students experience the world, and they put financial resources behind those opportunities.

When Leyden's school board president, Greg Ignoffo, speaks about the importance of supporting travel, he often cites a famous quote from Mark Twain:

> Travel is fatal to prejudice, bigotry, and narrow mindedness, and many of our people need it sorely on these accounts. Broad, wholesome, charitable views of men and things cannot be acquired by vegetating in one little corner of the earth all one's lifetime.
>
> (The Innocents Abroad, 1966) by Mark Twain

So how does this impact student voice? Emely Pazos graduated from West Leyden High School in 2017 and she had the opportunity to attend the global service learning trip to Mexico in her senior year. Dr. Polyak interviewed her to talk about her experience and the impact of that trip.

Along with her fellow students, Emely volunteered at the Casa Hogar orphanage in Puerto Vallarta, Mexico. She told the story of a little boy she met there, named Mateo. When all of the other children at the orphanage jumped up to get attention from the visitors from Leyden, Mateo hid under a table to avoid interaction. Rather than leaving him alone, Emely was persistent in trying to engage Mateo. She continually rolled a ball to him until he eventually started rolling it back to her.

Eventually Mateo opened up and began to trust and interact with Emely. She learned from the adults at the orphanage that Mateo's story included issues of neglect and abuse. Emely was determined to connect with him and show him that she cared about him. What she didn't expect was that her experience in that orphanage was helping her develop her voice and her potential direction for the rest of her life.

Emely went to college to pursue a degree in psychology and criminal justice. She wanted to help children who have been victims of abuse and neglect. When the Leyden Board of Education decided to support global service, they gave Emely an opportunity to discover her voice and ultimately make an immeasurable impact in the world.

The end of this chapter contains commentary from a Leyden graduate, Mike Motyka, who was able to participate in the global service learning trip to Peru in 2016. Similar to Emely, Mike discusses how this opportunity helped him find his voice and his place and direction in the world.

When the school board at Leyden decided to support global service learning trips, they also decided to support and have student representatives participate in the Global Leadership Summits hosted by Education First. Every year, Education First brings students together in destinations across the world.

In 2016, those students gathered at The Hague in the Netherlands to explore global human rights issues. In 2017, different students gathered in Italy to discuss the future of food for the world. The 2018 summit will be held in Berlin, Germany, to delve into the influence of technology on society.

For more information, visit: http://www.eftours.com/educational-tours/collections/student-summits.

These opportunities bring together student voice from across the world to help tackle the problems of our world today. At Leyden, the school board decided that their students' voices belong in those discussions and that their financial support furthers the development of student voice in helping their students make our world a better place.

The state of Illinois has taken notice in regard to the impact of global service learning. In 2017, a law was passed to create the Illinois Global Scholar Certificate. On its website, http://www.illinoisglobalscholar.org/, it outlines the importance of global service learning for students:

> Creating a global education certificate gives students an opportunity to examine current curricular offerings through a lens of global issues. This lens allows

students to make connections in their coursework and experiences that they might not otherwise make. Emphasizing global competence also prepares students to collaborate and compete in global contexts around the world and prepares students to succeed in a variety of fields beyond high school. Global learning leads to successful collaboration in scientific research, CTE, business, and STEM and enriches student understanding of the humanities, arts and language. Understanding the world should be an integral part of education in Illinois.

Student voice is something for us both to acknowledge and to nurture. This can happen on a global stage, but it can also happen locally. There are people who need help across the world and there are people who need help down the street. As educators, we have the opportunity to bring our students there; to help them provide service; and to help them discover their voice, their place in the world, and their place in their own communities.

This student voice can be developed locally through a variety of ways that don't even necessitate service learning. Districts are successfully creating student peer mediator programs that allow students to help each other resolve conflict. Schools are implementing peer mentor programs that allow students to use their experiences to speak into the lives of underclassmen as they grow and mature. And schools are allowing for student peer juries that help look at getting to the root cause of disciplinary situations so that their classmates can find success in the future.

When all fifty states, and all school districts within them, acknowledge this role and responsibility, we can truly change the world. We can maximize the power of student voice and use it to have generational change in our country and in our world.

ASK'EM

Ask: Who are the people in your school district who can help support service learning to influence the lives of your students? If you are thinking that your district might not support student voice on the school board, you'll never know unless you ask. As for finding interested students and seeking their input, that's the easy part—just ask.

Support: What resources can your district provide in terms of finances, time, and encouragement to allow students to experience service locally and throughout the world? Just like adults who are new to a school board, student members will need support and mentoring. After the first year, your outgoing student members can help them understand the role. You might also consider assigning adult board members as mentors for them to help with questions.

Know: As a school leader, you need to know what opportunities and programs exist in order to connect your students and enhance their educational experiences. You need to know that students who step up to the challenge of serving on a school board are also likely very involved. They have responsibilities for their coursework, sports, clubs, families, youth groups, and more. They are students first, and we need to make sure that service on the board does not detract from their ability to be successful in school.

Empower: When possible, students need to be empowered to determine how they want to serve. When they have voice in choosing their service, they are already invested in the outcome of their work. Make sure that your implementation moves beyond honoring students and actually empowers them to be contributing members of the board. Student voice isn't effective if you don't create a system to hear it and have the courage to listen to it.

Monitor: It is powerful to interview students after they have engaged in local and global service projects. This will help you understand the impact these opportunities have on their mind-sets, their voice, and the direction of their lives. As you implement student board members in your district, you will not likely get it perfect right away. Have conversations about how it is going, and be willing to monitor progress and make changes as necessary to get the best possible benefit.

SUMMARY

Ideas like including students on a school board and sending students overseas to do global service are likely to make any district a little nervous. It takes a certain level of trust and a willingness to take risks. The rewards come in the form of transformational leadership for a school district and transforming the lives and the life trajectories of your students.

The voices of students belong in those places, and it is incumbent upon school leaders to find ways to make that happen. When you empower students, it's easy to see the impact you have on them and on their lives. What you cannot measure is the ripple effect you will have on the people in their lives, the things they will do, and the effect they will have on the world.

GUEST COMMENTARY FROM RECENT
GRADUATE MIKE MOTYKA

Coming from a middle school with about 150 students (50 in each grade) and going into a high school with about ten times as many students, I barely knew who anyone was. I remember my first couple days of high school sitting in a classroom full of strangers and seeing random faces in the hallway. I knew that I wasn't going to live the high school experience sitting in silence and doing the same things every day, so I knew I had to get involved and step out of my comfort zone to change that feeling.

It was about a week into school, and after hearing announcements about club meetings, I knew that was my chance. I recall walking into a room full of upperclassmen and people I had never seen before. I quickly walked over to the table full of freshmen who I recognized and we sat there quietly not knowing what to do. Once the meeting started, the sponsor began giving out information and telling us details about what we would do in the club. It wasn't until then that I realized how fun this whole "involvement" thing can actually be.

After that day, I continued to go to that club meeting and realized that was what I want to do, so I joined about five more clubs that week. Getting involved in these clubs really opened up my horizons and gave me more opportunities. During my first year in high school, I was volunteering at marathons and 5ks, participating in beach cleanups and taking part in Leyden's annual Make a Difference Day. I began to get picked to be a part of certain clubs and to represent Leyden at leadership conferences.

As a freshman, I began to discover who I was and what I wanted to do with the rest of my high school experience. From the beginning, I made a purpose for my name and it opened up new doors for me to branch out into the person I am today. Freshmen year was a year of experiencing what high school had to offer and stepping out of my comfort zone, and I continued to do so for my years to come.

Sophomore year was a lot like freshman year with building and creating the person I wanted to be. I continued my passion for volunteering and getting involved with the school and community, but what really changed me that year was being a member of the peer leader group at Leyden. Peer leaders at Leyden is a small group of 10–20 students that are recommended by teachers and peers who are seen as natural leaders in the classroom, hallways, or even on the court or fields.

We were trained to be like mini counselors but with a student perspective. So we met with students 1:1 to guide and support them to improve on whatever problems they needed help with. Being a part of this group for the rest of high school really changed the way I thought of myself and others.

I grew a bond with other students that was just as close as a family would be. I began to create a selfless and passionate personality for what I did. It also gave me the opportunity to be part of life-changing situations for other people that really changed the way I thought about what I wanted to do with my life. Being chosen for this really put me down a path that changed my whole perspective on the rest of high school and what my future had in store.

Then junior year came around where, after one of my leadership team meetings, we watched a video on changing the school environment. Myself and a friend thought of not only impacting our school and community, but what if we did something for people less fortunate in another country. We brainstormed plenty of ideas and went to our principal, Jason Markey, to see what would be possible for us to do. It turned out that he was totally in favor of the idea and was already looking into programs where we could get involved in another country.

So, it was the summer before senior year when students (including myself) were given the opportunity to travel out of the country to Peru to work on a service project for low-income families. A group of about 30 of us worked with Peru's Challenge, an organization that helps stabilize families throughout Peru, to build a greenhouse for a large family. After building the greenhouse for this family, I don't think I've ever felt so satisfied and appreciated. The amount of love and gratitude we received from the family left us speechless. I am still speechless to this day because it's the greatest feeling knowing that what you did changed multiple lives forever.

Another thing that impacted me on this trip was visiting a local school that was recently built for the children in the area. When I walked through the gate into the courtyard, I had never felt something so special before. The amount of energy and endearment these kids had was unbelievable.

The kids gave us endless hugs, called us "amigos," and wanted to play with us the whole time. But the crazy thing is that some of these kids didn't have shoes, some wore the same clothes every day, and some might not have had three meals a day like most kids in America. It taught us all a lesson that we may take a lot of things for granted, and even with the little things in life, we should still find joy and appreciate what we have been given.

This trip was a life-changing opportunity that brought a new light to the person I am and the person I want to be. I learned so much about the lives of people in a third world country and also my own life here in America.

Going into my senior year after this experience inspired me to go out with a bang. I didn't want to take it easy this last year and settle down, instead I wanted to work hard and take every opportunity I could get. The Peru trip made me rethink the type of person I am. I can say that after going on that trip I started to appreciate a lot more and work a lot harder, because before the trip I was used to taking things for granted and having things handed to me. Since then, I have accomplished so much and couldn't be any more proud of the person I have become.

Toward the beginning of the year I was recognized by the district as "School Citizen of the Year" for working hard towards my goals and also following the Leyden motto: Be Kind, Find your Passion and Commit to Excellence. Then at graduation I was one of three students chosen to be recognized for my commitment to excellence. Having my story told in front of thousands of people left a huge impact on me because I've never felt more proud of myself for everything that I had worked for and accomplished in my high school career.

A few days before I left Leyden I was talking to my counselor about how sad it was leaving. I remember telling her that it blows my mind leaving the place where I discovered who I am. These past four years of my life have honestly been the best times of my life with great experiences and opportunities, but with the next four years and many years after that, I plan to make them even better.

Everything I've done in high school inspired me to go to college and major in psychology and neuroscience. After that I want to get my master's degree in school counseling and come back to Leyden to be a school counselor and athletic coach. Getting involved with many different things at Leyden really pushed me to want to come back because I want to continue the impact Leyden had on me with other students. My plan is to continue my passion to change the school and community environment by inspiring students to believe, strive, achieve, love, serve, give, receive, move, and drive for what they are capable of doing.

GUEST COMMENTARY FROM STUDENT SCHOOL BOARD MEMBER NOELLE LOWTHER

Personally, I loved being on the School Board. Of course, I would get the questions and jokes about whether or not the meetings were boring. Sometimes yes and sometimes no. Regardless of that, my senior year of high school was better because of my experience and I'm so glad that I decided to take it. Along the way, I have gained important knowledge and skills that will help me long after my life in high school. I grew as a person, increased my appreciation for School Boards, and made relationships that are going to last a lifetime.

Over the school year, I became a better leader and more self-confident. The position gave me more opportunity to share my voice and the students' voice. I am a very vocal person, but when you are talking with ten adults that you look up to, it can be an intimidating task. Although intimidating, having such responsibility was fun as I would share ideas and comments with the Board that really surprised or stumped them.

I was not afraid to be true to what students were telling me about our campuses. My public speaking skills grew with each meeting, conference, or event I went to. Even though I did a lot of talking, I have learned to become a better listener. I absorbed what Vanessa Gallegos, the other student Board member, was mentioning about the other campus and what the Board was talking about at a specific meeting.

Along with the listening, patience was to follow. Whether it was waiting for a request asked by students to be carried out or yearning for a long meeting to be done, I have become a more patient person.

With the up close and personal view that the position has, I have a truly renewed appreciation and love for the men and women behind School Boards. Only seeing a small portion of what Boards deal with, I can say that the students (or in the case of Leyden High Schools, the kids) are at the forefront of most meetings and discussions. Everything is done for them to better their educational opportunities. There are a lot of topics I didn't know Boards dealt with, such as residency issues.

I think that students don't see this part of Boards and automatically categorize them as authority figures, that one, make all the decisions, and two, don't know anything about high school (or school in general). After my "term" on the board, I can say parts of these comments are untrue. The Board does make serious decisions, but not without thoughtful deliberation. There is so much care because everything is done for the students. Many students think that the people behind a Board are unaware of high school problems.

The members that I interacted with in one way or another had a connection to Leyden. Whether their children went there or they taught at the high school level, Board members are well aware of the wants and needs of the students in the district. School Boards are serious business and should be appreciated.

I think my favorite aspect of being on the board was getting to know the Board members. From the first meeting to the last, I always felt welcomed and appreciated. They became my second family and they have (and probably always will) support me in all my endeavors.

Since there were so many cool experiences and opportunities that I was able to be a part of, I have met so many people along the way. The connections I made within the Board and district will always have a special place in my heart. I have already been ensured a teaching position at Leyden when I am ready!

Looking back on it, when I first decided to take the position, I didn't really think anything of it. I was super excited because I loved my high school, but I wasn't really sure what being on the Board meant. I don't think I really understood the capacity of the position until my graduation in May. It took me a whole school year to realize what I had been doing during the year.

Having both Dr. Polyak and the School Board president call Vanessa and I trailblazers put everything into perspective. Giving students the opportunity to share their voice is an amazing thing and should be considered more, as it offers insight into the Board and wonderful benefits to the students. For me, it was an amazing experience that has opened my eyes and allowed me to use my voice to better school and education, which I believe is the ultimate goal in the end.

Chapter 2

Building Our Community of Learners: Leverage Our Primary Conduit to Our Communities

I don't like when people say we need to prepare our students for the real world. The truth is some of them are experiencing more a "real world" that we will ever know. What we need to do is prepare them for a better world.

—Unknown (discovered on a tweet from Todd Whitaker)

The Reality of Community Service
The Possibilities
Purposeful Service
Student (Community) Leaders
Student-Driven Partnerships
Examples of Excellence
The Dilemma and the Ideal
Summary

Reflection Questions

Do our typical actions in school reflect our stated mission of creating community contributors?

Outside of the reason (excuse) of time, what prevents us from actively involving our students in our communities more often?

What prohibits us from having students sit on service-based committees and organizations such as Lions Club, Kiwanis, and the like while they are still students?

Would kids be more likely to engage in their communities if we gave them choice and allowed them to show us the purpose of the work?

Do you believe the more involved students are in their community, the more likely they are to return and/or stay involved when they are gainfully employed adults?

Stop-Think-Act

Stop: One of our primary purposes as a school is to create community contributors.

Think: We do little structurally to support this goal and even less to include students in the discussion of how we can do so in a way they find meaningful.

Act: Ask kids about how they want to engage in their own community. Their ideas, passion, and innovation make our jobs easy. We just have to get out of their way and provide them time.

THE REALITY OF COMMUNITY SERVICE

The mission statements of our three school districts are provided later in this section. Our guess is that when you compare our missions to the mission of your organization, there will be a great deal of similarity. As public service entities, our core purpose is to produce a citizenry that not only can maintain the current status of our community but also take it to new, never-before-reached heights of success, service, and prosperity.

Deerfield Public Schools District 109

To provide innovative educational experiences of the highest quality that engage, inspire, and empower each student to excel and contribute to improving the world.

Meridian Community Unit School District 223

To educate students to be self-directed learners, collaborative workers, complex thinkers, quality producers, and community contributors.

Leyden Community High School District 212

To educate, enrich, and empower students and communities.

Based upon what schools want to ultimately accomplish, as our mission statements often say, we do woefully little to directly address this end in mind. Everything done is in hopes that teaching students a subset of skills and facts will allow them to automatically transfer said knowledge and skills into the community setting.

Consider the following: Some schools encourage this, others mandate it, and some still ignore it. Very few schools are defined by service or work diligently to ensure that students view themselves as key contributors to society while in school. Moreover, schools almost universally fail to create this as a desired outcome.

Most kids in school that are completing service while in school will give you one of three answers as to why they are doing so:

- I need hours to graduate.
- I need hours to look good on college applications.
- I am being told to do so by a parent, coach, or faith-based organization.

Apparently, the belief is that we can force the behavior, and hopefully, that creates a new way of thinking for students. Covey's research on lasting change clearly presents that the key to lasting change is changing paradigms and then behavior will follow. Our challenge is: What are schools doing to intentionally and "pridefully" link their kids to their community?

Community organizations—School leaders are often expected to be visible in the community. If you are a principal or superintendent reading this, you have sat through your fair share of rubber chicken lunches at Lions Club, Rotary, Kiwanis, Optimists, and the like. You might attend as a community leader, and most likely you are able to biannually give some type of report based on what is taking place in the school or district.

Occasionally, the organization may ask for some help in terms of service from kids, but more often than that, the schools typically ask for financial support from the organization.

Internships, job shadowing, career counseling—most (high)schools have some component of this taking place in their schools. This work is generally for the few, not the general public, and is a result of one of two things. One is a concentrated effort to procure such a program by a proactive and engaged staff member. The other is a result of an organization or industry-at-large bringing forth a request to students.

Almost never is this an initiative led by students, nor is it something that typically extends to younger students. Kids have greatness within them. Think about just a few of the examples of kids doing wonderful things for their community.

Bagdad School, Bagdad, Arizona (Team Cottage Crafters): Family Career Community Leaders of America (FCCLA) and Skills USA students teamed up to apply their leadership skills to build a "sleeping cottage" for the homeless. Students planned, built, and delivered a complete tiny house to the Coalition for Compassion and Justice and the United Way in Prescott, Arizona. "Our hope is that we will spark a movement!" said students. See figure 2.1 for an example of a sleeping cottage.

The Phoenix School of Discovery, Louisville, Kentucky (Team R.I.S.E. [Refugees in a Safe Environment]): Team R.I.S.E. created a Bridge Building Day event to create cultural awareness and break down walls between cultures. More than 500 students formed teams and helped more than a dozen charities in the community while learning about and valuing each other.

The heartening aspect of these two programs is that they are meaningful, community-minded, and unmistakably aware of their communities.

Additionally, while these two programs were among those highlighted by the Lead2feed student leadership program, they are not close to being the only meaningful service projects our kids are taking on. The issue is that this excellence often exists in isolation. And worse—they often exist in spite of school programming.

Figure 2.1 Example of FCCLA Sleeping Cottage

To explain, at schools we often discuss how we want community-minded students, but we keep them at school until 3:30 p.m., many middle and high school–aged students have athletics or activities until 6:00 p.m., and they have two hours of homework when they get home because they need to take high level and advanced placement classes to stay competitive.

Oh, and make sure you are well rounded, have a meaningful relationship with your family and friends, and enjoy "the best years of your life." And, when you are done with that, knock out a bunch of community service in your spare time. The issue is that what we say is important to us is not often reflected in the conditions and circumstances that we place upon our students.

THE POSSIBILITIES

When something is important to us, we make it part of what we do in schools. A great example of this would be to attend a Leader in Me school. See figure 2.2 for a brief description of the Leader in Me outcomes. The 7 Habits of Mind become a way of life. In doing so, it impacts language and lessons, and it is given the most valuable resource in schools—time. The possibilities for successful student leadership in our communities are endless, if we allow it be a part of school time.

Teaching Students 21st Century Leadership and Life Skills

When Principal Muriel Summers asked parents and business leaders what they wanted in their schools, what she heard reinforced what most people believe—that our schools should not merely be focused on improving test scores, but should provide opportunities for students to develop their full potential.

- Leadership
- Responsibility
- Accountability
- Problem Solving
- Adaptability
- Communication
- Initiative and Self-Direction
- Creativity
- Cross-Cultural Skills
- Teamwork

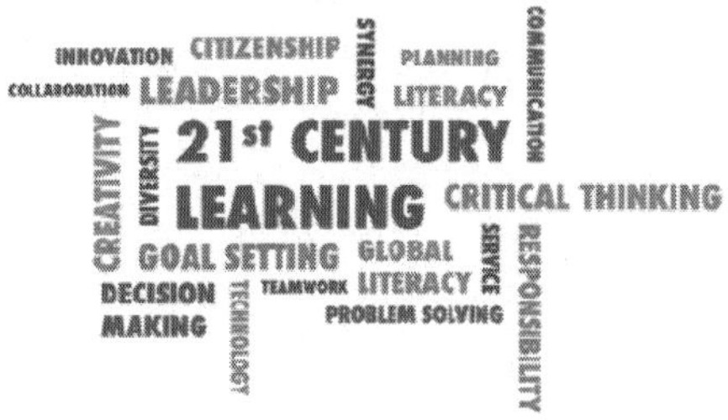

Figure 2.2 Leader in Me (Franklin Covey)

Think of the possibilities. Consider what could be done if an average-sized high school of 500 students dedicated one full day to service per student as part of the curriculum. That is 3,500 hours of service for a community over the course of a year at the cost of around 0.6 percent of the potential maximum instructional time for kids. This is an average of three minutes of instruction per day that is lost to make a monumental difference and demonstrate to students that we mean what we say and we truly want to work toward our stated missions.

With time, and student voice, all things are possible. Consider the no-cost initiatives that could be used to replace the tired, half-hearted attempts to involve students in our community as described earlier.

PURPOSEFUL SERVICE

Great results come when a group of people organize around a particular theme or event that is important to them. Identify your specific purpose and let that drive actions. Think about fund-raising in its broadest sense and from a personal perspective. Are you more likely to donate to the Red Cross today or the day after a hurricane hits the coast of Florida? Are you more likely to donate blood at one of the (probably) ten blood drives within driving distance this month or the day after a significant tragedy?

The examples used are extreme, but it bears out that proximity, context, and reliability to a particular event can often drive sacrifice and service. This is usually lost on schools and lost in the decision-making process.

Having a group of student leaders organize behind one particular purpose to funnel effort, energy, and enthusiasm toward a cause has the possibility to create meaningful change and momentum toward service. Do you think volunteering to do a roadside cleanup one Saturday per quarter will instill a service mind-set in a student the same way helping to build a ramp in a house for a disabled school volunteer would? Of course, it would not—context and personalization matter.

Yet, in schools, we often try to promote service so much that we create a culture where kids jump through hoops to get the right amount of hours and totally forget and/or ignore the purpose behind what they are doing. We strongly believe that school leaders need to create a system where this does not occur. The only possible way for this to evolve and significantly change is by increasing the voice of students in the process.

A handful of excited and committed students can galvanize a service effort far greater than any mandate or cord worn at graduation ever could. Allowing student voice and unifying service efforts under one collective umbrella allow students to take part in something that truly is transformational for the community and has a much greater possibility of being transformational for the student.

The cost is allowing student voice and not prohibiting the use of school time for service.

STUDENT (COMMUNITY) LEADERS

As described in this book, numerous schools are taking steps to ensure that student voice is heard by including students on their governing boards. A natural precursor and/or extension to this practice is to include students on community boards and within community organizations. It is no secret that the average age for members of service organizations is increasing.

These service organizations play vital roles in the community, and we are confident that many of you reading this book donate your time, effort, and energy to one or many of the great civic organizations. These organizations do simply spectacular work, but many of them are aging significantly. Personally, we are members of organizations in particular where we are fifteen to twenty years younger than the *average* age of membership. Membership is a huge issue for these clubs.

Some organizations reach out and try to partner with schools to spread the message of service and connection to community. Prominent junior clubs are Key Club, a subsidiary of Kiwanis Club; Interact, the junior group to the Rotary; and Leos, the school-based partner to the Lions Club. The issue is that the continuity seems to stop there. Far too few members are "graduating" from Leos to become Lions. It appears as though our students see the organizations as somewhat disconnected.

It is possible, though, that with greater investment in youth-affiliated clubs and perhaps college/university outreach, these young members will revisit their membership as they enter the workforce. Somehow, we should ask students in clubs, like Interact, Leos, and Key Club, for example, what would it take to go from a high school club member to an adult member later in life.

This is precisely why schools should sponsor students to be members of all community organizations. There are innumerable benefits that could occur as a result of this type of initiative.

Below is a quick list of just a few of the benefits:

- Community members hear what school is really like
- Students create professional networks while in high school
- A clear connection to a lifetime of service is established
- Potential parent memberships to the same club would fill a missing demographic in most of those organizations
- Students learn to communicate and interact effectively with people in different age groups

The costs are possible membership fees to clubs or organizations and time.

STUDENT-DRIVEN PARTNERSHIPS

It is also not a secret that most schools and districts do not create an experience that is a direct line to being successful in the workforce. Some would challenge that is not the true point of primary and secondary education, but it is impossible to contend that better partnerships would not benefit our students.

When we work with principals and ask them for goals and priorities for the year, strengthening partnerships and creating opportunities in the community for students are almost universally mentioned (irrespective of the success of current partnerships or programming).

However, it is generally in the "it would be nice to get there" pile. The actual practice of working hard to create opportunities, during normal school hours, for kids to experience what life in the workforce is like and to gain requisite skills for employability is generally lacking.

This begs the question, why do we leave it to ourselves, the adults in the room, to create these partnerships? Imagine a class where the intended outcome for each student was to connect with a local business and create an internship plan for the future.

Imagine a class where students select the local businesses they value and would like to partner with. Imagine a class where students do not see geography as the ultimate limit to whom they can connect with and form partnerships deeper and more valuable than the adults could have ever imagined. This is all a distinct possibility if we set the vision and let go.

We can design a curriculum focused on providing students the communication skills necessary to interact with desired third parties and recruiting them to be part of a unique partnership. Next, the students would need to work through the complexities of establishing an internship plan for either themselves or a future generation of students that provides value to both the student and third-party organization while understanding the constraints that come along with being a student.

This process alone, before any direct work is done for the third party, could provide relevant real-world skills that would lead to eventual gainful employment for a student than most anything we currently provide in schools.

The costs are the effort to reimagine what preparing students for the real world looks like and time

EXAMPLES OF EXCELLENCE

The incubator program believes that the solution to America's economic issues is to continue to build business within our country. This program's curriculum focuses on providing students the skills to do just that in the traditional high school setting. Proponents of this program point to data from millennials noting that over 90 percent of millennials (a large percentage of the parents of the students we now serve) believe teaching entrepreneurship to be important.

The program relies heavily on the involvement of local business leaders to add to and diversify the curriculum and to act as coaches as students continue to develop requisite skills. The incubator program (http://incubatoredu.org/) started in Illinois and is now in over ten states nationwide and growing.

Platt High School, Connecticut–Platt High School partnered with O&G Industries, Connecticut's largest privately held construction company, to provide hands-on experience and help kids connect in a different way to their school. O&G and the school constructed a nine-month experiential learning curriculum for high school students.

The program consisted of a behind-the-scenes look at the construction of their own school, and allowed students to gain experience, earn credits, and learn hands-on about careers in construction. As a result of this partnership, O&G received the Midstate Chamber of Commerce's Innovation in Education award for the O&G Builds program at Platt High School in Meriden.

Career Education Associates of North Central Illinois (CEANCI)—In northwest Illinois, a vocational cooperative holds business roundtables each month to support curriculum evolution and development for teachers. This program systematically places teachers of trades in roundtables with the future employers of students taking those classes. These roundtables have resoundingly provided the "why" for curricular change.

Additionally, this has allowed for great partnerships that have been leveraged in a number of ways to provide a more holistic product for students. While this is currently more of an adult-oriented group, we believe student members would produce an improved learner-centered synergy.

THE DILEMMA AND THE IDEAL

The biggest dilemma to seeking student voice on how they can better engage in the community and correspondingly make a difference in their own life is that we often view improvements or change in the school setting as a zero-sum game when it comes to time. There are lots of great things schools would like to incorporate; the issue is that with every great idea, something must correspondingly leave the typical practice of the school.

Occasionally, this attrition is a wonderful thing as an antiquated concept or initiative steeped in tradition but lacking in effectiveness or relevance leaves our schools. Let's assume, however, there is a school in which every single instructional minute is leveraged and capitalized on to its fullest possible value—then what?

This is typically where student engagement in the community falls: as a nice idea that is not quite nice enough to crack the "rotation" of concepts embedded in the curriculum. Such ideas are generally placed as an after-school club or activity, and little change occurs. Little change takes place because the students who would have engaged civically without any club are the ones who do so through the clubs. The students who had never imagined themselves a community leader or contributor continue to sit on the sidelines. This is precisely why something must change in how we envision what school "looks like" and what it needs to provide our students.

This is where the ideal situation presents itself as the best possible option. Embedding community leadership into existing curricular structures presents an opportunity to leverage the most precious resource in schools—*time*.

Additionally, curricular-based initiatives have the ability to impact more students just based on the number of student contacts that take place in the classroom compared to any other possibility of engagement. This is real work and takes real time, but as a school leader or teacher reading this book, this is our clearest path at creating substantive change that is systematic, and in most cases, we have a significant modicum of control.

Community partnerships are naturally win-wins. Oftentimes, our community partners receive the best possible resource in these arrangements—human resources. When students have the opportunity to earn credit while learning business or trade skills, it is a benefit on many levels. There is a disconnect between what industry needs in its employees, what students envision the workforce to be, and the skills provided by traditional school curriculum. Imagining this as a Venn diagram, the circles barely overlap.

The opportunity exists, if we listen to our students and community partners, to create a Venn diagram with a great deal of overlap that better serves our students. Leadership opportunities exist in great abundance for our students in our communities if we redesign our concept of what a student leader looks like and what role they serve. The days of our best student leaders being satiated with leadership experiences that consist of planning dances are well behind us. We must work with our communities to allow the tremendous potential of our students to be unleashed and work to improve our communities.

Kids are naturally engaged and desire to improve their communities. Schools often imagine this as a sell. It is not. Instead, all that needs to be done is to listen and to lift the perceived veil that exists between what kids can do in school and what kids can do to truly make a difference.

Time is the perceived barrier to engaging our students in our community. The value placed on every possible second of instructional time has created a massive dilemma in schools. If the best possible solution is not found (integration of community engagement and leadership) into the curriculum, then there is no time for it at all. Removing this self-inflicted, arbitrary, and honestly arrogant protection of instructional time to allow students to tell us what work in their world they find meaningful and engaging would do a substantive amount to improve our schools.

ASK'EM

Ask: Schools and school leaders should start by asking themselves a handful of questions. Questions such as: When do we take the time to ask students what is important and meaningful in their world? Do we ever ask them whom they would like to help? Does any part of our curriculum allow for students to truly connect with our local community? Asking ourselves these questions will allow us to ask very similar and powerful questions of the same type to our students.

Support: Kids will most likely want to bite off more than they can chew when it comes to connecting with and engaging in their local communities. This is awesome and what makes student voice so special and the catalyst to true school improvement! When students dream big, we must be very intentional about not crushing their dreams because of our past failures. Remember, when you do not think it can be done, simply Google "student leads community service event " or "student demonstrates civic leadership," and see the plethora of responses you will receive.

Know: It is important to know that this aspect of seeking student voice may not breed the immediate response that some other areas may. Students may not have dreamed big in this area. Students may not have seen themselves as an agent of service and community leadership. Know that your students have this in them, but know that we may have to work to help them see themselves and their potential for greater than they currently do.

Empower: The best thing we can do for our students is to get them in positions of leadership, collaboration, and work experience with other adults. Intentionally and systematically demonstrating that schools believe in students and see the purpose of schooling as something that extends beyond the physical walls of school is incredibly empowering. Great schools and school leaders help students to see their place in society and their place as a student in their school as something larger than a passive recipient of lessons and knowledge.

Monitor: The purpose of engaging students in our community is multifaceted. The benefit to the students should be tangible. They should grow in leadership experience and in life and trade skills that help them to be employable in the future. The benefit to the community should be an infusion of new ideas and human capital to continue to improve the circumstances of others. The benefit to the school would be an increased community presence, improving leaders, and a more relevant school experience for students. This all sounds great, but engaging students in our communities is not something that is ever "done." It will take constant monitoring and attention to ensure that our students are growing at their maximum capacity and giving back to our communities.

SUMMARY

For too long, schools have talked a great game when it comes to servicing their communities and their desire to create community contributors out of our students when our actions have said otherwise. The game changer when it comes to creating a school or a district that truly serves its community is to understand the value of time. Schools systematically protect time in a manner that prevents creative connections to the community and often discourage community collaboration.

This chapter is meant to illuminate that issue and to encourage schools to press forward to achieve their mission of creating community-minded individuals. This starts with an open mind and open ears to listen to students and learn from how they want to connect with the community in potentially different ways than we would have imagined as adults. In part II that follows, the focus will shift to student voice in technology instruction. In chapter 3, we emphasize student voice in digital citizenship, and in chapter 4, we address the 1:1 transformation.

Part II

STUDENT VOICE IN TECHNOLOGY INSTRUCTION

Chapter 3

From Digital Natives
to Digital Citizens

The notion of "digital citizenship" is so messy. All the more reason educators have to be in on these conversations with students.

—George Couros, Author

Just Because They Are Digital Natives Does Not Mean They Know How to Act Online
Elevating Student Voice—Making It Invaluable
Find Resources and Define Digital Citizenship
Student Leadership and Partnership
Summary
Guest Commentary from High School Student Kyla Guru

Reflection Questions

In what ways are students part of decision-making processes in your system?
How has your digital citizenship curriculum scope and sequence changed in the past few years?
Where will you look for resources on how to engage students in your planning and policy review?

Stop-Think-Act

Stop: How did you develop your current (if you have one) digital citizenship curriculum?
Think: Have you asked students what they think—truly think—about the latest instructional planning around digital citizenship?
Act: Leverage student input to create a revamped and meaningful digital citizenship curriculum that will meaningfully impact student decision making and actions.

JUST BECAUSE THEY ARE DIGITAL NATIVES DOES NOT MEAN THEY KNOW HOW TO ACT ONLINE

Adults are quick to point out missteps of students online and issue blame, but schools are lacking comprehensive and engaging digital citizenship curricula that meet the ever-changing needs of our students.

The 2016 State of the States second annual report on K–12 broadband connectivity shows that 75 percent of all students in America are connected to high-speed broadband (retrieved from https://www.educationsuperhighway.org/blog/2016-state-of-the-states-report-governors-and-internet-service-providers-are-driving-dramatic-progress-in-connecting-americas-k-12-students-to-high-speed-broadband/). In addition, with the increase in 1:1 initiatives where students get their own technology devices for school and home usage, the need for direct instruction on digital citizenship is greater today than it has ever been before.

Educators recognize the importance of digital citizenship. Issues such as cyberbullying, sexting, and other inappropriate behaviors taking place online are pervasive in society and are undoubtedly impacting students' lives and thereby the overall function of schools. While quick to point out the struggles that occur as a result of inappropriate online behaviors and poor digital citizenship, many schools are offering little substantive attention on how to best teach the important skill of digital citizenship. In essence, we complain about the problem but often provide no solution.

Moreover, when schools do make this an area of emphasis, far too few are engaging students constructively in any element of the dialogue. Students are not engaged in the planning, as an information resource as to areas that need attention from their perspective, or in the evaluation of the instruction they are receiving. It is simply wrong *and* an enormous missed opportunity that students are often overlooked as consultants in the digital citizenship conversation and programming.

ELEVATING STUDENT VOICE—MAKING IT INVALUABLE

A recent review of the Deerfield Public Schools District 109 BrightBytes Technology and Learning survey data from March 2017 shows that students get most of their digital citizenship knowledge from their parents or teachers. See figure 3.1. The assumption is that adult values and "commonsense" adult mores and norms somehow automatically transfer into child decision making and actions in the digital world.

There is one major elephant in the room not being addressed, however. What happens when their parents and even teachers do not know what to teach? This is a great reminder of a quote often attributed to Stephen Covey:

 Student sources of advice about responsible Internet and cellular phone usage

Deerfield Sd 109

FRAMEWORK: Technology & Learning
DOMAIN: Classroom

DATA FROM: Jan 1, 2017 To Jun 30, 2017

SUCCESS INDICATOR: Student Digital Citizenship

VARIABLE: Student Sources Of Internet And Cell Usage Advice

1st
89%
Parents/Guardians

2nd
81%
Teachers or other adults at school

3rd
35%
Coaches or Community Members

4th
31%
Librarians

5th
25%
Family Members

6th
19%
Friends or Schoolmates

7th
13%
Websites

8th
3%
Nobody

Why This Matters

As schools increasingly adopt 1:1 initiatives, teachers and students "must understand digital citizenship and the issues it entails" (Kiker as quoted in Ribble, 2012).

Citation
Ribble, M. (2012). Digital citizenship for educational change. "Kappa Delta Pi Record, 48," 148-151.

Figure 3.1 Student Source of Learning about Digital Citizenship

"You cannot teach what you don't know; you cannot lead where you will not go."

Ignorance when it comes to online safety and digital citizenship is simply the reality for many parents and staff members who are wading through these murky waters as digital immigrants. Thus, as educators and leaders, we must acknowledge that a gap currently exists between the behaviors we want from students and what is being exhibited and chart a course to help teach students, parents, and teachers about digital citizenship.

Our experiences have shown the value of seeking student voice and acting on their input through the use of surveys. Survey students—sounds easy, but how? With whom? What survey? The trick is surveying students and using their voice strategically, meaningfully, and on their behalf. This means we must do something with the results in addition to making pretty charts and graphs!

An example is using a partnership with a research team or building a survey in-house with students and teachers as designers. This allows leaders to seek out direct input and voice from students regarding their understanding and implementation of digital citizenship strategies. For example, instead of assuming what digital citizenship needs your students have, find out and discover.

From a recent local survey, 89 percent of students seek guidance from parents and guardians about digital safety. Are schools teaching parents and guardians what digital citizenship is? Student voice informs reality. Take the time to ask.

Once you find out from where and from whom students are learning, leadership can take steps to support their needs and meet them in their reality. When leaders know what reality is, they can empower parents, staff, and students with information and guidance. We have found that taking steps immediately can lead to changed culture and inclusive student voice in decision making. Start to ask, start to measure, and start to do. We have used all or parts of these examples and suggestions in our current and past practices as systems leaders.

FIND RESOURCES AND DEFINE DIGITAL CITIZENSHIP

Use a strategic or deliberate information-gathering process like surveying students to find out what their voice/reality is. Convene a focus group of students, and simply ask questions about digital citizenship: Have you ever been cyberbullied? What does that mean? Do you know what to do if you are bothered online? We should look to sources such as Common Sense Media or other school districts that have implemented successful programs.

Our leadership lessons have taught us that it's best to limit focus on no more than five key areas. Use the student focus group responses and survey your students and staff; take the input and prepare an immediate curriculum plan and a parent education program. From the data and student voice, make action plans and enlist all hands on deck—including students to teach lessons about what digital citizenship is and how to best address it.

Focus on defining digital citizenship, making a plan for data gathering, and teaching, following up with postworkshop surveys. There will likely be resistance about opening up social media sites. Some staff will feel this will lead to problems for students, other staff, and the overall environment. Adults tend to consider the worst-case scenarios, scenarios that are dark and nefarious. The reality is that most students, especially younger students, are not jaded, dark, or predisposed toward law breaking or creating and distributing lewd content.

Another argument can and will be made that teachers cannot be expected to master content area knowledge, pedagogy, brain science, and so on, and, on top of that, be on the cutting edge of technology. The reality is we are not asking staff to become cybersecurity experts; we're asking them to teach citizenship. The reality of the world we live in, however, is that social media and continued technological advancements are not going away.

People were resistant to e-mail in the late 1990s and cynical about the Internet just fifteen years ago, and look where we are today. Educators, whose primary purpose is to construct experiences that prepare kids for our ever-changing world, have no choice but to keep up with technology. Simply put, technology is not something people are artificially using to change schools—it is a tool that has and continues to fundamentally change society. We simply have no choice but to embrace this shift or be left behind.

STUDENT LEADERSHIP AND PARTNERSHIP

"We cannot trust kids to lead on this topic" is an example of a traditional and fixed mind-set. Ceding authority or control in any area can be difficult. Doing so in an area you have not mastered is even more troubling. As adults, we simply cannot do this on our own as this is often not our area of expertise. In fact, there is quite possibly nothing that we should trust our kids with more. As digital natives, our students are in the best possible position to help guide adults through the minefield of digital citizenry.

From author Dr. Jason Ohler, "If we don't ask students to help frame the system, they tend to game the system. We all know that students can be incredibly clever when it comes to circumventing the Internet rules we put in place. However, when students have a voice in creating the rules, they're not so quick to game them" (retrieved from https://www.bigdealbook.com/blog/?show=activities_to_give_students_a_voice_in_the_digital_citizen ship_conversation).

In the Deerfield Public Schools District 109, when Mike became superintendent on July 1, 2013, he unblocked Twitter. The #engage109 hashtag was born soon after, and the DPS109 digital transition had begun. The district partnered with BrightBytes to conduct research about the impact of the transition to digital learning. One of the largest areas of need as reported in the first administration of the BrightBytes survey was about teaching students how to act respectfully online.

See figure 3.2 where the 2017 data are compared with the 2014 data. As a result of student voice and input, they are taught how to act respectfully online 10 percent more today than in 2014. In addition to the students being taught how to act respectfully online, the time spent per year teaching about cyberbullying has increased since 2014. The increase in time spent shows that the needs increased and so did the response.

Throughout the book, we incorporate *ASK'EM* to emphasize the point that if you intend to elevate student voice from invisible or superficial to invaluable, or meaningful, you simply have to "ask'em." In this chapter, we provide two ASK'EM areas as we're thinking of meaningful ways you can start to ask 'em what they need, want, and can do.

Ask—Ask through surveys. Build your own, get them from a free source or partner, or make a partnership with a company or group. But remember, surveys are only as good as the actions their results drive. See figure 3.3 for an example survey you can use today.

Support—Support the community with parent and student workshops. Schedule parent workshops to teach the parents what the data show. In the parent education programming, have students present as well. Student voice is also putting students at the forefront of the education program.

Know—Know what digital citizenship topics to add to the curriculum. There are lessons for free and for purchase that address topics of relevance and interest. Topics can include creating an online identity, how to build a digital footprint, how to vet sources, and more.

Empower—Empower your community of learners and create a culture of trust. Unblock any sites like Twitter, Facebook, or Instagram. Teach the students how to use these services (if of appropriate age); allow staff to use these services responsibly. Create a culture of trust and a culture of yes.

Students are taught how to act respectfully online

Deerfield Sd 109

FRAMEWORK: Technology & Learning

DOMAIN: Classroom

SUCCESS INDICATOR: Student Digital Citizenship

VARIABLE: Student Frequency Of Learning Digital Citizenship

DATA FROM: Jan 1, 2017 To Jun 30, 2017

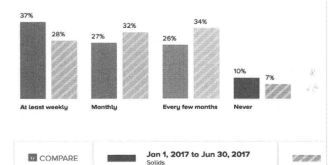

At least weekly: 37% / 28%	Monthly: 27% / 32%	Every few months: 26% / 34%	Never: 10% / 7%

 COMPARE

 **Jan 1, 2017 to Jun 30, 2017** Solids

Why This Matters

"Instead of restricting access, we should educate young people to participate [in the digital world] responsibly, ethically, and safely. Through proper use of social networking sites, students learn social media etiquette and cultivate their digital citizenship" (Wang et al., 2013).

Citation
Wang, S., Hsu, H., & Green, S. (2013). Using social networking sites to facilitate teaching and learning in the science classroom. "Science Scope, 36"(7), 74-80.

ⓘ DATA HIGHLIGHT **64%** of students are taught this on a regular basis

Why This Matters

"Instead of restricting access, we should educate young people to participate [in the digital world] responsibly, ethically, and safely. Through proper use of social networking sites, students learn social media etiquette and cultivate their digital citizenship" (Wang et al., 2013).

Citation
Wang, S., Hsu, H., & Green, S. (2013). Using social networking sites to facilitate teaching and learning in the science classroom. "Science Scope, 36"(7), 74-80.

Figure 3.2 Students Taught How to Be Responsible Online

What social media apps do you use regularly? (circle all that apply)
 a. Instagram; b. Snapchat; c. Twitter; d. Facebook; e. Other
Who is talking to you about Internet safety? (circle all that apply)
 a. Nobody; b. School staff members; c. Parents; d. Some other adult
Has an adult talked to you specifically about? (circle all that apply)
 a. Internet safety; b. Privacy concerns; c. Impact on relationships;
 d. Cyberbullying; e. Self-image; f. Information literacy; g. Creative credit/
 Copyright
What areas do you want to learn more about? (circle all that apply)
 a. Internet safety; b. Privacy concerns; c. Impact on relationships;
 d. Cyberbullying; e. Self-image; f. Information literacy; g. Creative credit/
 Copyright
Which areas cause you or your friends the most "stress" or "drama"? (circle
 all that apply) a. Internet safety; b. Privacy concerns; c. Impact on
 relationships; d. Cyberbullying; e. Self-image; f. Information literacy;
 g. Creative credit/Copyright
Rank the following as the most beneficial ways to learn about the following
 topics: a. Peer mentor; b. Specific classroom lessons; c. Assemblies;
 d. Other

Figure 3.3 Sample Survey

Monitor—Monitor the impact of digital citizenship and education. Make a
 decision on what metrics matter when it comes to digital citizenship. Some
 schools may be concerned with quantifying the impact on the number of
 bullying investigations; others may focus on student engagement, while
 others will look for examples of students utilizing appropriate and legiti-
 mate online sources for argument formation. There is not a right or wrong
 answer—but there should be a goal associated with this effort. Ideally,
 the goal will link directly to the data collected through the initial student
 voice survey.
Ask—Do we as adults "get it"—are we on the right track with our efforts?
 (Students are honest.)
Support—The teachers, students, and parents—get resources (free or for
 purchase), ask the leadership team to help.
Know—Who are your students? Do you really know what their interests are?
 Do you know what their digital citizenship needs are? Communicate and
 publicize the results of the surveys to establish a common understanding
 and language.
Empower—Your students can become teachers, and your teachers can
 become the staff developers and the community developers. Teach

sessions like Twitter for Parents, Raising Digital Citizens, The Rules of Social Media, Growing Up in the Digital Age, Creating a Digital Footprint, and more.

Social media is ever-evolving and cannot be controlled, so STOP trying. This makes it incredibly scary for adults. Additionally, those adults not actively using social media to connect with other educators and leveraging it as a tool for their own professional growth may struggle to see the utility in this learning tool.

Once educators understand that social media can be used for connecting (beyond pictures of relatives in other states) and growth—they will (start to) embrace the platform. Additionally, it is perfectly acceptable to "call out" the fear. Once professionals talk about everything they are afraid of, they will realize that those fears should exist with or without new platforms being blocked or not.

As a school community of leaders, it is our duty to expose kids to the risks and rewards the real world presents for them. Our job is not to shelter students from their reality when they are not within the confines of school-administered Wi-Fi.

Monitor—Check your efforts again—this is a process not an event. Monitor the impact of the training (i.e., discipline referrals, friendship group success, police intervention, perception surveys).

SUMMARY

With the increase in 1:1 initiatives where students get their own technology devices for school and home usage, the need for direct instruction on digital citizenship is greater today than it has ever been before. Since students get most of their digital citizenship knowledge from their parents or teachers, we as school leaders need to determine what to do when their parents and teachers don't know what to teach.

In 2014, the Deerfield Public Schools went 1:1, and with help from students, parents, teachers, and administrators, they produced a handbook that included the subject of digital citizenship. Their move to 1:1 transformational learning had a foundation of digital citizenship built in. From the DPS109 1:1 Parent/Student Handbook, available at www.dps109.org.

Digital Citizenship

School-issued devices should be used for educational purposes. Students are to adhere to the Authorization for Electronic Network Access, which every family signs upon entering District 109. Students will adhere and agree to the following:

- *Respect yourself.* I will show respect for myself through my actions. I will select online names that are appropriate. I will use caution with the information, images, and other media that I post and view online. I will carefully consider what personal information I post.
- *Respect others.* I will show respect for others. I will not use electronic mediums to antagonize or bully others.
- *Protect yourself.* I will ensure that the information, images, and materials I post online will not put me at risk. I will not publish my personal details, contact details, or a schedule of my activities. I will report any attacks or inappropriate behavior directed at me while online. I will protect my passwords, accounts and resources.
- *Protect others.* I will protect others by reporting abuse and not forwarding inappropriate materials or communications.

We started the chapter with the problem statement: Adults are quick to point out missteps of students online and issue blame, but schools are lacking comprehensive and engaging digital citizenship curricula that meet the ever-changing needs of our students. The answer is found in student voice. Digital citizenship involves social skills and life skills citizenship training too. Creating a culture of awareness and prevention throughout the school can be an important step in lowering incident rates of unsafe online practices. Following the suggestions and the ASK'EM plan will make a positive and measurable impact on digital citizenship.

Inviting students to speak at parent education sessions, student workshops and assemblies, and other training sessions will make a positive step. As seen in figure 3.4, the keynote presenter at a parent education program on digital citizenship is a student.

Ask the students what they know, do, and think. Beyond the focus group and survey—don't stop there—keep the conversation going. Use the ASK'EM strategy.

Although teaching digital citizenship is a noble endeavor and one that should make sense considering the abundance of technology in society, change in and of itself is often met with resistance. Some teachers will not feel it is their job or responsibility. Anticipating and planning for challenges and obstacles will help advance the success of digital citizenship lessons. Common fears may fall into one of several areas, including expertise, keeping up, peer influence, fear, and time.

In chapter 4: Student Learning through 1:1 Initiatives, we will address the why in the transition to 1:1 environments. We'll also explore differentiated instruction, expert views, as well as how student voice can be woven into

Opening Session: SMS Learning Commons
• *BrightBytes Data on Digital Citizenship in 109 (Mike)*
• *Nearpod Lessons for Adults on Digital Citizenship (Marcie)*
• **The Student Perspective (Kyla Guru)**

Session 1 (7:35–8)	Room	Session 2 (8:05–8:30)	Room
Twitter for parents (Mike + Jeff + Dave)	309		
Raising digital citizens (Marcie + Ann Buch)	307	Social media inclusion/exclusion (Lisa Markarian + Ali Chroman)	307
The rules of social media —13 means 13, modeling good behavior (Cathy + Scott + Anthony)	308	Fostering conversations with your child—Botvin Redux (Cathy + Megan)	308
Growing up in the digital age—both sessions (Kyla Guru)	Library	Growing up in the digital age— both sessions (Kyla Guru)	Library
Creating a positive digital footprint—Middle School Focused (Maria Galanis + Sam Kurtz)	310	Protecting child's identity (Adam L + Del. Steve Petorelli)	310

Figure 3.4 Agenda for Workshop with Student Keynote

the decision-making processes. Before we start chapter 4, however, we have chosen to end this chapter with a commentary written by high school student Kyla Guru. Miss Guru also happens to be the keynote speaker highlighted in figure 3.4.

GUEST COMMENTARY FROM HIGH SCHOOL STUDENT KYLA GURU

Childhood in the 1990s was inchoate. Kids learned to swing on the swing-set, read fairy tales, and sat quietly while *Home Alone* played on the VHS. If snowflakes or rain fell outside, they would be honored to stomp out the door and mark their footprints. Today, from the minute that a child is born, they are instantly connected to a universal data labyrinth. They are welcomed into their grand digital playgrounds, listening to audio books of fairytales before bedtime and using VR to stand with Kevin in a scene of *Home Alone*.

From the minute they wear their footies, their digital footprints are sculpted by their every step through technology. But there's nothing to fear, because this is how it is meant to be. The development of mankind has perennially relied on progression. Sure, early homosapiens did not know about Artificial Intelligence or Machine Learning. But certainly, if they did, they would urge that the only direction for mankind to progress in is upwards and onwards. Therefore, two things are for certain: Our decisions will be driven by technology, and technology, while empowering, is equally vulnerable.

The next generation cannot be burdened with an untimely malware while using biotechnology to cure cancer. The future generation cannot jeopardize confidential data to ransomware attacks while building the rocket taking us to Mars. Those to come cannot face a major breach in the Cloud while constructing our first smart cities. The face of tomorrow, filled with surprises and possibilities with technology, will inevitably require our children to wear their "white hats" and fluently speak the language of cybersecurity. I know that we need to start now.

By 2020, there stands an estimated 4.17 billion Internet users and 34 billion devices, including IoT. With this, comes more risk, more vulnerability, more possible loss, and more facets we must hold accountable. Over 1 million cyberattacks hack small businesses, trusted corporations, government facilities, hospitals, and even personal devices daily. Our corporate governance in economic sectors must work tirelessly to protect themselves from incoming attacks. As this is the reality, I envisioned a future where the youth of our generation develops these devices, drives the IoT expansion, and manipulates real-time data at their fingertips.

They will have to visualize and mitigate cyberattacks both personally and in the workforce. The need for youth to pilot the exponential growth of IoT was the primary inspiration behind Bits N' Bytes Cybersecurity Education. How did I begin? It was all passion. In June 2016, I was named one of the thirty participants in the exclusive NSA-sponsored GenCyber Training Camp at Purdue University. After this instruction, outside of the classroom, I began self-learning computer systems and became familiar with user-vulnerability. As a result of my early exposure to technology and seeing cyber-defense come alive, cybersecurity soon became a passion of mine.

Additionally, I always held an affinity for outreach and leadership growing up. Since age 7, I have taken summer engineering classes at Northwestern University, fueling my natural entrepreneurial spirit and flare for letting my voice for change be heard. In 2015, I received the Prudential Spirit of the Community Award and the President's Gold Medal Volunteer Award from President Obama for my work towards combating world hunger. As a result, I was further motivated to think of ways to blend my two seemingly dissimilar fervors: cybersecurity and outreach. I knew that my passion would be the root of service and the mantra of how I would lead my community.

Next, I saw a need in society. While attending South Park Elementary School, I saw technology begin to integrate with classroom instruction. During my first grade year in 2008, students were first exposed to devices. Now, every student has their own chromebook to take home every day. Just like this, according to PBS, 74% of teachers in America say technology allows better reinforcement of content, while motivating students as well.

Seeing this learning blossom before my eyes, I began to ponder on the importance of internet safety. As a high schooler, it was not uncommon to see reckless behavior on social media, over text message, or while surfing the web. I had a thought: what if I could teach our digital natives the tenets of cyber security at the youngest age? This way, I theorized, they could carry these lessons with them as they progressed through upper level education, equipped to handle cyber-situations.

Recognizing this desire, I contacted Deerfield Mayor Harriet Rosenthal with the interest of joining a cyber-task force in the neighborhood. I was surprised to hear that we lacked one, especially since just the previous year, our educators experienced the identity theft of their Social Security information. I then realized although that the community had much initiative for engaging digital natives in technological enterprises, skills like detecting phishing, downloading safe apps, and reading privacy policies were skills not emphasized through school curricula. Students were vulnerable to online risks, and were not familiar to face the challenges.

With my knowledge, passion, and eagerness to learn and change the world, I began my journey of cybersecurity advocacy. I began organizing meetings with the principals of District 109 schools. Eventually, Dr. David Sherman, the Principal of South Park Elementary, commissioned me to produce a tutorial teaching digital awareness concepts for classrooms to view. From this point, my initiative launched. I wrote, produced, animated, directed, and narrated a short film explaining the importance of cultivating a safe digital environment where students can succeed, premiering it during a tech-talk I organized with the South Park staff.

In addition, during Hour of Code Week, I visited South Park School and Kipling Elementary School, helping students complete coding activities and explaining my initiative. After my debut at South Park Elementary, I formed a partnership with district technology coordinator Mrs. Marcie Faust and began to produce more films, teaching a total of 3,015 students as the cartoon alias "Detective Safety."

Seeing the impact this project had on the students of just one district, I became the founder of Bits N' Bytes Cybersecurity Education, a cybersecurity educational initiative. In order to reach more districts and families,

I designed my website (www.bitsnbytes.us.com). Here, I share news about the ever-changing cybersecurity spectrum, daily tips, and weekly lessons for educators, parents, and students. To communicate on a massive scale, I started a Bits N' Bytes Twitter page (@GuruDetective) where I shared my blog posts with many districts throughout Illinois. In addition, I also brought my initiative to Deerfield High School, developing the CyberSmarts Training Package App in my AP Computer Science Class, where students practice detecting phishing emails and making strong passwords.

On February 23rd, 2017, Bits N' Bytes collaborated with DPS109 during Digital Learning Day to ask students to pledge safe online practices. Together, we organized an event where students would watch my latest film, use my app, play educational activities, and take the pledge on our website. We urged teachers to tweet the lessons for their classrooms by offering prizes for the schools with most pledges.

We received a phenomenal response from Twitter and 735 student pledges in Deerfield. However, this was not the end of my efforts. I displayed my films with over 200 high school students, speaking about the importance of privacy and safety on digital interfaces. Subsequently, I took a leadership position in organizing a Day of Cyber-Education on April 12th, 2017 in association with the district technology board, hoping to educate the 5,000–6,000 parents of the district.

As the keynote speaker, I spoke about my project with the schools, sharing my perspective as a high-schooler, and educating parents about how to begin cybersecurity education early. At this point, I could see how I was speaking volumes: because of the unique perspective I was able to bring as a high-schooler in the digital culture and environment of my peers.

I was able to influence parents that even though the Internet can be a risky place, we cannot be *scared* of data; we simply must protect it and share safe practices with our students. Overall, I had impacted more than 75% of Deerfield's estimated population of 18,476, as well as families outside of Deerfield.

My leadership as a student has brought me to schools where I have presented to auditoriums full of students. One presentation occurred at Kaneland Harter Middle School to a group of 6th and 7th graders. I had presented to a group of teachers weeks before at an edCamp, and one had contacted me, interested in a partnership with the school. I eagerly agreed and began planning the event, setting up interactive activities covering data privacy, password protection, phishing detection, and digital citizenship.

For instance, I had the students Google themselves in the data privacy station to show how much about their families, personal lives, and academic lives is available free online. Then, they self-directed themselves to ask the next question: what can we do to reduce the amount of data that can land itself in the hands of possibly malevolent people? In one hour alone, the students began forming these thought-provoking ideas and beginning to rethink their digital behavior. There, I realized that young students are merely more unaware than we presume.

However, when given the information in a stimulating way, they are eager to learn more! That night, I began spreading the word on my blog that education was necessary for our most vulnerable, providing my ideas and resources for making practices routine in the classroom.

Since I wanted to cater to the most vulnerable citizens throughout the community, I saw another population that my initiative needed to impact: Senior citizens. I began communicating with the local senior homes, the Whitehall of Deerfield and the Patty Turner Center in order to hold one "Cyber-training" class for the seniors and move forward from there.

Currently, I am organizing for my upcoming event at the Patty Turner Center on July 14th, with an estimated 50 senior attendees in mind. With this project, I knew I needed to publicize the event in all the avenues I could in order to get the best turnout, from printing fliers to posting on social media, and even contacting the Mayor of Deerfield to get the word out. It was necessary for me to quickly utilize business-level organization and communication skills as a freshman in high school in order to plan for the best results. From this point, I plan for increased sessions, as well as establishing a system of daily tip sharing for the seniors.

I envision a widespread movement for cyber-security awareness. These past few months of educating cybersafety have started a passion project for me that I will continue to develop through high school. I plan to partner with more local libraries as well as more districts in order to further expand my reaches. With these partners, I plan to expand Bits N' Bytes and post more weekly blogs, research and write about relevant topics that educators want to hear, continue producing films, and tweet tailored daily tips, news, articles, and games to assure that families and followers see cyber-safety as an importance everyday.

My goal is to form a group of passionate young students to help organize these events and advocate for digital safety in their classrooms, selecting and educating ambassadors from each grade to help promote the cause directly. Lastly, my long-term goal for the end of this year is to utilize my connections at NIU and Michigan State and reach out to the Chicago Public Schools.

With my partnership, I hope that the schools are able to begin and continue to immerse their students in the necessary education for the cyber-future. Through edCamps, parent nights, senior cyber-talks, and interactive tech-talks, my leadership has taken me far beyond the reaches I could have imagined when beginning this project.

For my work in leading this initiative and this movement, I have been honored by Stanford University's #include Fellowship, the Optimist Club of Deerfield, and the National Center for Women Information Technology. As a result of being selected as a She++ #include fellow this year, I received an all-expense paid trip to the Silicon Valley, where I presented my initiative to representatives from Facebook, Google, GoDaddy, and Stanford University in the beginning of April.

Here is where I received more fuel for my projects: I saw how women leadership in STEM was utterly necessary. I also have been invited to speak at the Deerfield Village Board Meeting and have been interviewed by the Deerfield Review, featured in Reigning It's Women Who Reign Campaign, and recognized by my high school administration. Seeing my work, I was chosen as my district's ambassador this year for the Hugh O'Brien Youth Leadership Conference, another incredible experience where I learned about my leadership style, and how to increase synergy. Here is also where I learned that being a leader is about leveraging your strengths to take part in something bigger than yourself. It's not only for those who are great public speakers or outgoing. A leader can lead in different ways.

The way I lead demonstrates my qualities coming together: my giving nature combined with passion and enthusiasm. With all of the inspiring people I met, the places I got to travel just in my freshman year, and the experiences I gathered, I felt the leader in me develop and highlight itself.

Since the beginning of this venture, I have learned about myself as a leader while developing the skills I will utilize in the workforce. Communication, enterprise, collaboration, adaptability, and grit are a few of the leadership qualities that have become my character. I was able to find myself while bringing initiative to the community. After my projects began, data shows that the educators of District 109 became more knowledgeable about creating an online presence, as the numbers towards "High" and "Very High" trend upward, both seeing 2–3% increases.

Also, DPS109 saw a 3–4% increase of students that were both taught how to act respectfully online and how to safely share information. This increase occurred over just 4 months of implementation of my program and partnership. I realized that it's important to make a lasting impact on the world regarding topics that affect them the most—this is pretty easy with persistence and planning! If we turn our passions into service to the betterment of the world, we instantly become leaders in movements. Now and in the future, there will be innumerable amounts of solutions necessary to problems. If we are forward-thinkers, fearless and unafraid of commitment, solutions can be sought.

My goal was, and still is, to increase awareness within students, educators, and seniors (the youngest and oldest members of society) about safety on the

World Wide Web. I wanted others to reflect on their regular habits online and the responsibilities that come with them. As a young leader, I took a leap of faith, determined to raise cyber-awareness with both the youngest and oldest members of society. What was the result? I allowed many to grow comfortable and knowledgeable about protecting themselves and their loved ones against the safety issues that arise with the upcoming digital era.

The key is to be fearless, be the one to shake the Director's hand at a seminar and introduce yourself with pride, and to know that your perspective is valued and, if applied, can be used to make great change in any arena of your passion. If you stand by this cause, those around you will support you and help create a positive synergy around your project. For instance, months into my project, my school received a phishing email attack on educator accounts—emails that were socially engineered to sway the district into clicking on the "Google Docs" link.

This occurrence highlighted the relevancy of my project and not only teachers, but teenagers began to support my movement. This support, for a young entrepreneur, speaks volumes for the project's development. Student leadership is the most inspiring and groundbreaking kind, and we need it now more than ever. In my case, if we get a stronghold over these fundamentals of safety and security of data online, we unlock a whole new world of possibilities for the child, who can then bring their own change to the world.

Why is this important? Childhood in the 2030s will be incredibly progressive. Kids will create inventive playgrounds with their robotic friends, fly drones above their head to turn off their lights before bedtime, and spontaneously 3D print their popcorn for the running of an old time classic, *Home Alone*. Life will be a whole new terrain, but our digital citizens, knowledgeable and powerful, will be prepared.

Chapter 4

Student Learning through 1:1 Initiatives

The greatest challenge of the day is: how to bring about a revolution of the heart, a revolution which has to start with each one of us.

—Dorothy Day

The Move to 1:1—Views from Experts
Student Voice Should Be Used to Ensure Tech Initiatives Are Learning Initiatives
How Can a Site Visit Influence Decision Making?
How Are Students Engaged in the Decision-Making Process? How Do Students Help Make Material Decisions? It Is More Than Device Selection and Management—Examples from Practice
Summary

Reflection Questions

At what stage in a 1:1 transformation is your system? In what ways are you measuring the impact of the transformation?
Is your transition to a 1:1 environment viewed as a technology initiative or a learning initiative?
With your transition to a 1:1 environment, how was the student perspective in learning considered?

Stop-Think-Act

Stop: Where will you look for resources on how to engage students in your planning and policy review?
Think: In what ways are students part of decision-making processes in your system?
Act: Form focus groups of students at each grade level to learn how the transition to 1:1 is going (or will go based upon their interests).

THE MOVE TO 1:1—VIEWS FROM EXPERTS

The most progressive and easy-to-observe transition into the 21st century for schools is the concept of putting devices into the hands of students. This chapter explores how implementation of this initiative can be maximized by engaging students in the conversation about what they need to best maximize their learning.

One-to-one computer initiatives have been in place since the late 1990s, and in 2002, the state of Maine put forth its one laptop for every child program. Duran and Herold (2016) write about recent research studies and their findings:

> The researchers also looked beyond test scores, reviewing 86 additional studies that did include an empirical examination of 1-to-1 laptop initiatives' impact in K-12 schools, but did not include an experimental design and/or quantitative results. Among the findings from that review:

- A 1-to-1 laptop environment often led to increased frequency and breadth of student technology use, typically for writing, Internet research, note-taking, completing assignments, and reading.
- Students used laptops extensively throughout the writing process, expanding the genres and formats of their work to include writing for email, chats, blogs, wikis, and the like.
- Student-centered, individualized, and project-based learning appeared to increase in at least some instances of 1-to-1 laptop rollouts.
- Student-teacher communications (via email and Google docs, for example) and parental involvement in their children's school work increased in some instances.
- Students expressed "very positive" attitudes about using laptops in the classroom, as findings consistently showed higher student engagement, motivation, and persistence when laptops were deployed to all students.
- Students' technology and problem-solving skills improved and their ownership of their own learning increased, according to some evidence.
- There were mixed findings on whether 1-to-1 laptop programs helped overcome inequities among students and schools.

Those results should be interpreted with caution, the researchers said, because they "tended to rely on observation, survey, and interview data."

One notable point is that the researchers' commentary is centered around the impact on students, the work of the students, and the education of the students. As the movement in modern education moves from teacher centered to learner centered, it's consistent with current trends and those which we espouse in this book.

Marcinek (2015) lays out effective ways systems can implement 1:1 transformation. Notable is the commentary from "Audrey R." (p. 28), a seventh-grade student, who offers her perspectives about the change from nontech to high-tech learning environments. The fact is that Marcinek includes student voice in his "how to" book is powerful in and of itself and is emblematic of our entire focus in this book: student voice is real, powerful, and quite easy to access. From *Unlearning Leader: Leading for Tomorrow's Schools Today*, in chapter 6 section on 1–1 A Brief Look at Going 1:1:

> As Andrew Marcinek writes in his book, *The 1:1 Roadmap Setting the Course for Innovation in Education*:
> "Technology is more than just 'Computer Class;' it is a literacy that must be threaded throughout the fabric of a school. In a 1:1 environment, you're preparing students to be responsible citizens of the physical and digital worlds. But it's easy to get overwhelmed with devices; you have to have a plan for technology that keeps learning at center stage."

Marcinek's point regarding keeping the focus on learning cannot be lost in the rush to embrace EdTech as a panacea. Though we are strong advocates for instructional change as the catalyst for a substantive change in student outcomes, content is as important as instruction in the classroom. We are also advocates for informed student-centered change. Like George Couros and others, we are not "data driven," instead we are student driven.

Our entire premise is that getting data with and from students is imperative for sustained learner-centered transformation. Transforming learning environments from analog to digital, another way of describing a 1:1 initiative, goes far beyond device acquisition and deployment. We believe that all learning decisions should (and can) involve some degree of student voice and input.

Beyond the devices, the training, the measures, the voice for whom the 1:1 move is made is the students; in what ways are students involved in the decision-making process? In the next section, we'll share ways in which students can be engaged in authentic, invaluable decision making. As mentioned in chapter 3, digital citizenship is as relevant today as civics instruction regarding the democratic government structures.

The world in which our children (and adults) reside is more and more digital each and every day. Just like we cannot expect children will become good citizens because they are citizens (without teaching), we cannot expect they will become good digital citizens just because we go 1:1. In Mike's district, the move to 1:1 took place over many years of study and review.

In 2013, when his leadership team was in place, they were charged with the task of "going 1:1." With innovation grants for teachers and with surveys to students, parents, teachers, and administrators, they were able to study and analyze a multimonth innovation plan before recommending to the Board of Education in March 2014 that they "go 1:1." In the sections that follow, we'll share examples of how leadership and change decisions have been incorporating student voice into the digital transformation.

STUDENT VOICE SHOULD BE USED TO ENSURE TECH
INITIATIVES ARE LEARNING INITIATIVES

In moving to a 1:1 educational program, we found including students throughout the transformation process will yield greater impact and overall success. For example, whenever change is planned in a school system and multistakeholder groups are convened, we argue that a student group *must* always be incorporated. Students are the receivers of education—let's not do education to them; let's do education with them.

All of us, young and old, are limited in our view/vision by what we know and have done. We are a sum of our experiences. Often it is most challenging to elicit change desires from the students who only know what they know. Stated differently, it's tough for students to automatically share vision and inspiration for the future when the 19th-century school system is all they know in most instances.

It is necessary for adults—teachers and leaders—to facilitate learning environments where we teach students to develop and change their vision of themselves, their school, and society. We must offer opportunities for real debate and discourse where we treat students as valuable partners, not as inconvenient participants.

Too often we have seen students, the primary clients in the education business, are either ignored outright with decision making or are seen as inconvenient players. Typically, student voice is truly listened to and respected only on relatively inconsequential topics and pushed aside when something "important" comes up.

In our experiences, however, when student voice is sought out, analyzed, incorporated, supported, and validated, the pedagogical and structural changes have far greater impact. Because it works and it has worked in our systems, we believe that students should be part of device selection and review as well as pedagogy review and change in any system.

At Leyden High School District in Franklin Park, Illinois, Technology Director Bryan Weinert looks to the students when it's time for device selection. The school district is a 1:1 Chromebook district with approximately 3,500 students. The year before the district plans to purchase new devices, Bryan buys samples of the devices that are currently available on the market. Those devices are then given to current students who use them for a week.

Bryan could simply meet with those students to get their feedback; however, he takes it a step further. He asks the students to write professional reviews of the devices and give recommendations about whether or not they would be a good selection for the district. He then posts those reviews online. As a result, student voice drives the district's device selection. An unexpected result is that school districts across the country started reading those student reviews and using that information to inform their purchases. When you think about it, who is better to recommend what devices kids should use than kids themselves?

How can this be done in your district? The first part of change is the hardest part. The "DO" part of the Plan-Do-Study-Act method is often the trickiest. As educators, we're really good at planning and forming committees. We're pretty good at studying. What the world has not often seen much of, though we are seeing more and more through our research and practice, is doing and acting. See figure 4.1 for a look at the planning process Plan-Do-Study-Act.

Often the first step is for the leader to ask students to join in. Ask their parents to accompany them whether they are five years old or fifteen years old. The inclusion of meaningful student voice can also have positive effects on community engagement and broader messaging and communication. Once the devices are selected, the workshops are planned, and the 1:1 school year is in force, be sure to plan for monthly or quarterly check-ins with your multistakeholder team that includes students.

Students have had education done to them for many years. Let's do education with them. When technology, or anything new, is introduced into the learning environment, we implore you: "don't assume the kids want or understand the changes." Often folks say or think that "digital natives" love

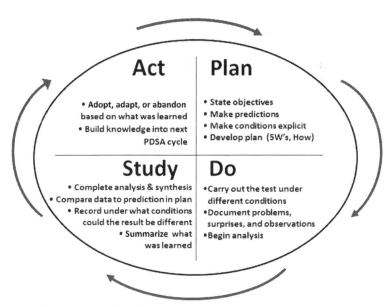

Figure 4.1 Plan-Do-Study-Act Visual

technology and immediately know what to do once the classroom becomes tech infused. Did anyone ask the students? Did anyone involve them in the planning and thought processes? Did anyone make their voices invaluable instead of invisible?

HOW CAN A SITE VISIT INFLUENCE DECISION MAKING?

This chapter is about student learning through 1:1 initiatives. Beyond the literature and study of 1:1 transformation and transition, we have also used site visits to amplify learning and decision making. In order for the move to 1:1 to focus on and impact student learning, our teams have made it a priority to visit students during authentic learning and teaching. The 1:1 instructional transformation should have an immediate, profound, and forever effect on teaching and learning. Site visits are part of a team investigating the ins, outs, ups, downs, successes, challenges, and so on involved in a multiyear rollout leading to a 1:1 learning initiative.

In addition to seeking student voice directly from the students in our own districts, there is tremendous value in traveling outside of your own district on site visits. On these visits, there are usually observations of students, question and answer with students on panels, and the incorporation of student voice throughout.

Below are Mike's notes from one of the early visits his team took:

What struck me and the other members of the team during our visit to classrooms in South Berwyn School District 100 today was ENGAGEMENT in the learning process. From multi-station math centers to one computer per group cooperative literature groups, to a blogging middle school class, each and every student was observably engaged in the learning. We were able to ask students questions, "How's it going?," "Do you like this type of learning?," "What are you learning today?," "What would you tell us that is helpful . . . etc.?"

To a student, from age 6 to age 14, they clearly knew the learning targets, they got "the point" of the lesson. They used their devices as naturally as we used books, folders, paper notebooks, and trapper keepers. The students willingly identified that they enjoyed learning with technology, they enjoy using eChalk, and they find it relatively easy to use the equipment at school and at home. Even though 76% of the students in SD100 fall into a low-income category, the students and the district officials indicated that home internet access is higher than 95%.

The world changed . . . we are preparing young people for THEIR world . . . we are not preparing them for our past . . . the experiences in South Berwyn today support the value of transforming education (teaching and learning) as we prepare students for their (present) and future. In the 1:1 learning environment, students get learning assignments in class (and at home) from their teacher's online lesson plan (in eChalk). The teacher uploads (attaches) documents, videos, materials, etc. to the eChalk site and the students access the materials online.

An example was shown in a 4th grade classroom where the students were interacting with "The Gallon Man." The students were working in cooperative groups with one computer per group, the students had the teacher's instructions on a video so they could listen to the instructions as many times as they wanted.

The students were also cutting with scissors and construction paper, pasting and gluing with glue, and creating a "Gallon Man." The lesson was ENGAGING. All students were working on listening, speaking, cooperating, creating, etc. Technology was a tool in the lesson; learning was the focus.

See figure 4.2 for a look at a "Gallon Man."

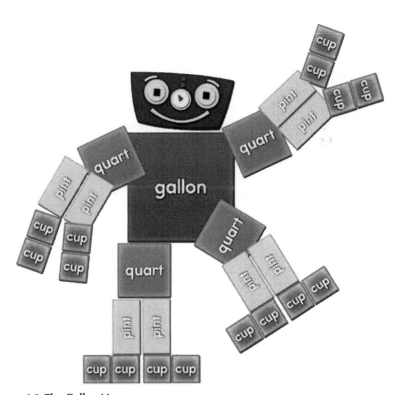

Figure 4.2 The Gallon Man

These notes were rewritten and focused on the content for this chapter—adapted from a blog post Mike wrote in October 2013 (retrieved from http://dps109supt.edublogs.org/2013/10/01/reflections-from-a-site-visit-11-learning-environment).

HOW ARE STUDENTS ENGAGED IN THE DECISION-MAKING PROCESS? HOW DO STUDENTS HELP MAKE MATERIAL DECISIONS? IT IS MORE THAN DEVICE SELECTION AND MANAGEMENT—EXAMPLES FROM PRACTICE

In Mike's district, they have been engaged in full-scale 1:1 transformative educational environments since 2014. The first instance of student voice in this process came from student surveys during the Innovation Grant 1.0 multimonth review process. Subsequent to the actual move to 1:1, the district partnered with a research partner to get benchmark data that could show growth and areas for improvement.

Students, along with parents, teachers, and administrators, have been surveyed about their knowledge, understanding, application, and improvement in many areas. These areas include the use of the 4Cs (Communication, Collaboration, Creativity, and Critical thinking), digital citizenship, access at home and school, and multiple skills and opinions. As an example, in figure 4.3, the differences in student collection and data analysis from 2014 to 2017 are shown.

The use of data, and the use from the student voice specifically, allows the district to make informed decisions with true voice and objective information. In figure 4.4, there is evidence of a disconnect between student and teacher perceptions about the frequency students are asked to identify and solve authentic problems. Forty-four percent of students report that they are asked to solve authentic problems weekly compared to 29 percent of teachers reporting that on a weekly basis, students are asked to solve authentic problems.

This type of data allows the school leaders to form questions of inquiry as to why there is a discrepancy. Perhaps it is because students have many teachers in a week's time and even if some of them allow for weekly problem solving, other teachers don't. It could also reflect a gap between perception and actual work. Either way it opens up the possibility of data-informed dialogue.

In 2016, the Deerfield teaching and learning and technology departments set off on a year-long evaluation, study, review, and recommendation phase regarding multiple aspects of the 1:1 experience. The technology review committee was made up of teachers, administrators, and students. In addition to

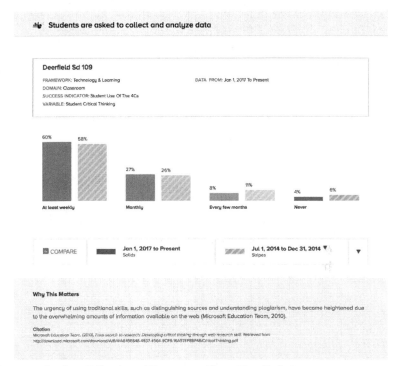

Figure 4.3 Student Collection of Data over a Three-Year Period

pouring over the survey data, the teams also met in person, conducted walk-through visits of the classrooms, and engaged in real planning and decision making.

There was a team of students on a "STAT" (Student Technology Assessment Team). These students participated in walk-through observations of each school and virtually every classroom. They have been making student voice invaluable in their transformative learning environment transition. Their perspectives were shared equally at the "table" with teachers and administrators in contemplating what was working with the 1:1 move and what could still be improved.

Excerpts of the findings and the January 2017 report from the committee, including student members, are shared in tables 4.1 and 4.2.

In figure 4.5, we are sharing the individual committee member opinions on recommended Promethean board replacement. Values indicate percentage of committee members' preferences.

The entire change process in Mike's district has been marked by their hallmark of holistic change. This type of change involves listening to multiple stakeholders including student's voices. Holistic change is becoming the norm.

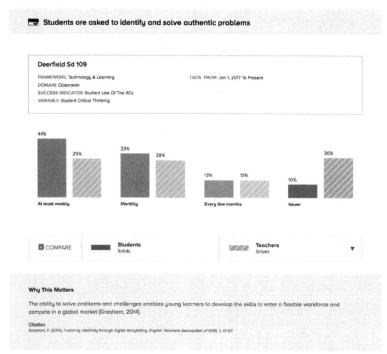

Figure 4.4 Frequency of Authentic Problem Solving (Teacher/Student Comparison)

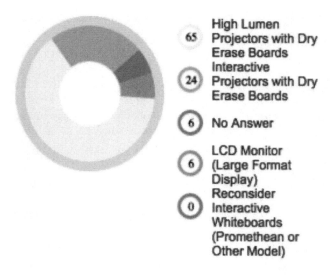

Figure 4.5 Individual Committee Member Opinions on Recommended Promethean Board Replacement

Table 4.1   What Should Student Devices Be Able to Do?

Photo/Video	Easy access to info
	Take pictures/video manipulate
	Efficient use for student creates content
	Front-facing and rear camera
	Be able to seamlessly connect to digital display (screen, projector, etc.)
Typing	Efficient—touch or physical
	Long-lasting, durable, portable device that isn't limited by operating system or current apps (upgradable)
Flexibility	Creation
	Promote collaboration
	4Cs
	Touchscreen movie making
	Picture—front and back camera
	Word processing
	Capability to present to others
	Keyboard if necessary
Support for Learning	Allow participation, creation, collaboration
	Be fast, responsive, reliable, flexible
	Be able to work with multiple platforms
	Accessible from home
	Safe need for keyboard option (physical/nonscreen)
	Durable
	Allow manipulation, ease of manipulation
	Camera, video, touch, versatile
	Ease of tech support—allow students to explore questions, and interact with the world—create content, explore content—collaborate on many different levels
	Photos, videos
	Word processing/writing tool
	Allow student-choice
	Multifunctional (interact with apps—i.e., See-Saw)
	Interdisciplinary
Internet Access	Google functionality
	Multimedia creation and consumption (functional dual-facing camera that is easily manipulated) 1:1 (single user)
	Word processing
	Multiple ways to document the learning process (suite of tools) Durable ability to capture sketched content
	Option to connect accessories (keyboard, headphones)

Table 4.2 If We Change from Promethean/ActivInspire, What Will Be the Concerns from Teachers?

General Concerns	Fear of Change	Needs
"I" have spent too much time over the years creating "my" FlipCharts.—"I" need something to replace "my" ActivInspire software.—"I" need a pen at the front.	Panic, loss of curriculum in the software, won't get proper PD, teachers don't know other options, new options need to be taught while old still available.	Differentiated PD teachers being able to use flipcharts.
Teachers have put in many hours of work creating flipcharts and some are concerned that all of that work will be lost.	Insecurity with new technology. Need effective, meaningful training that can be implemented immediately. Teachers need tools (i.e., effective stylus pencils). This is a huge change; will take time for teachers to adjust. Are Chromebook teachers at a disadvantage not being able to mirror work?	People need to understand *why* ActiveInspire might not be the best program for our students anymore. Teachers need to be taught different methods to move instruction away from the front of the classroom and really question the rationale for "interactive whiteboards." PD needs to be differentiated for individual teacher needs.
Flipcharts Interactivity— especially in the younger grades.	Change is scary. Some people will be devastated by change no matter what, while others will thrive. I truly believe that if we offer job-embedded, just in time PD *that all staff will be successful, even through the fear*.	ActivInspire lessons need to be re-created/transferred. If we go with a short-throw projector some teachers may need markerboards/whiteboards installed in their rooms as they have a chalkboard or a wall behind their current Promethean board. Let's make the change!
There is an argument for special education populations, K-1 and math, to keep interactivity and others to go to just lumen projectors.	I think they are afraid of change. That they will lose their flipcharts and have to re-create lessons.	Losing what they have not knowing how to replace what they use it for with what is available training on whatever the replacement is

(Continued)

Table 4.2 (Continued)

General Concerns	Fear of Change	Needs
Loss of flipcharts/ content they have put large chunks of time into creating—loss of ease of interaction (young students with fine motor issues cannot interact on an iPad as easily as they can on the board)— needing PD on new resources (they may know about them, but haven't used them in this way)	Loss of content created over the years. Lack of familiarity with how new options can be used to deliver content. Lack of time to build new content.	Math teachers will find difficulty moving from their ActivInspire even within a year and a half or more. There is an argument that maybe they can still have this as an option within their specific classrooms. This way we are meeting specific teachers and student needs. In order to teach math, there needs to be some direct instruction alongside with something that is interactive.
They will be concerned with the time spent on making flipcharts and wanting to keep them. Those that use the interactive charts will want to know what they will use instead. Will there be PD?		
I think teachers will be concerned that they will not be able to transfer their flipcharts or be given the tools to do so effectively.		

In Bullis, Filippi, and Lubelfeld (2016, p. 54), they identify three main bullet points about components of high-impact holistic change in place in the Deerfield Public Schools:

- Inspire. Motivate teachers, students, and community members to dream big. Lead with data, energy, emotion, and hope. Encourage teams to produce tangible results through dream/do leadership.
- Engage. Facilitate stakeholder group planning, review, and implementation recommendations.

- Reinvest. Lead analysis of the change process. Encourage stakeholders to benchmark results of change against growth targets, and set goals for continued growth.

Involving students as key players in the review of a massive initiative like 1:1 impact review is inspiring. As a school leader, taking the time to participate in committee meetings, visit school classrooms during real instructional time, and debriefing and sharing results is engaging in the process and empowerment of students.

Reinvestment takes place when the process yields results and the processes are made public and transparent. Students were expected to complete the same data analysis form as the teachers; their voices were as important as every other member of the walk-through team. See table 4.3 for a look at the data analysis protocol.

ASK'EM

Ask: Allow your team to become immersed in available evidence whether it comes in the form of research, case studies, site visits, or a combination of the above. Always seek input to learn from others, the aim is to replicate that which works and learn to avoid others' pitfalls.

Support: Teams that include students show the support for student voice with action. Offer teams support in the form of time, resources, guidance, direction, and empowerment.

Know: Begin with the end in mind. Have an idea of where you want to go with all initiatives, including the move to 1:1 learning. Know what you want so if you get it, you can continue and replicate. More importantly,

Table 4.3 Data Analysis Protocol for the Tech Review Committee

Step 1	What parts of this data catch your attention? Just the facts.	(five minutes: two minutes silently writing individual observations; three minutes discussing as a group)
Step 2	What does the data tell us? What does the data not tell us?	(five minutes: two minutes silently making notes; three minutes discussing as a group) Make inferences about the data supported with evidence from the data.
Step 3	What are our key conclusions? What recommendations does the team have for addressing any problems/issues?	(five minutes: two minutes silently writing individual observations; three minutes discussing as a group)

know that if you are not getting the outcomes you sought, it's time to change gears.

Empower: Empower students. Truly empower them to stand side by side with teachers, administrators, parents, and community members as authentic change agents. Follow models woven throughout this book as examples of how to bring the voice of all children to the boardroom.

Monitor: Be sure to monitor the impact of your actions. For 1:1 transformative environments, there needs to be some sort of measure. Whether it's anecdotal, part of formal research, or tied to other measures, some form of measure and follow-up is essential in any program or initiative.

In chapter 7, we'll take a look at personalized learning. Our approaches will be similar to those in the last chapter. We'll look at expert views and definitions of the topics, and we will show why student voice is essential in the change process. Finally, we'll share the "how" to get student voice from invisible to invaluable in the larger macro view of personalized learning.

SUMMARY

In this chapter, we looked at how student voice can be used to ensure tech initiatives are learning initiatives. We shared perspectives on the move to 1:1 from experts. We shared an example of how our students engaged in the decision-making process. We explored examples of inclusion of students into multistakeholder teams to help make material decisions.

The implementation of the STAT team, the student voice at each step of the 1:1 review process and projector replacement process, made the student voices equal to the adult voices. The process also allowed students to present to the Board of Education. The voice of the student transitioned from invisible to invaluable!

In the next section of the book, part III: Student Voice in Design and Communication, we'll look at facility and learning space design, instructional learning (personalized learning), as well as communications and public relations. As shared in the 2016 School Voice Report (Quaglia et al., 2016), and as demonstrated in the text of our book,

> We have learned that a process that honors the voices of others simultaneously fosters respect, creates lasting partnerships built on trust, and develops a sense of shared responsibility. (p. 7)

This sense of shared responsibility is essential when taking student voice from invisible to invaluable!

Part III

STUDENT VOICE IN DESIGN AND COMMUNICATION

Chapter 5

School Design/Structures: What Is School?

> Putting student voices at the center of everything we do will help us design the future with them and for them.
>
> —Lubelfeld and Polyak (2016)

Reflection Questions

When you view your schools, do they look like workplaces or prisons or factories? Why? In what ways have you been reviewing the design of learning spaces?

With learner-centered approaches and personalized learning gaining popularity, in what ways are you designing or redesigning learning spaces to reflect these concepts?

How have or will students be involved in the transformation and redesign of learning spaces?

Stop-Think-Act

Stop: Do you remember what your favorite classroom or learning space looked like? Do you have learning spaces from the past or for the future?

Think: In what ways have you designed your office or your learning spaces that can be replicated in your schools? Have you ever asked occupational therapists about the needs of the students in terms of furniture?

Act: Do an informal survey of your students and teachers and ask them if they find the "physical plant" most conducive to learning, and then address their commentary.

THE CEMETERY EFFECT

In their recently published book, Murray and Sheninger (2017) spend some text regarding the concept and subject of designing learner-centered spaces (see chapter 4: Student Learning through 1:1 Initiatives). In a June 2017 article for EduTopia, entitled "Rebooting Industrial Era Seating," they compare traditional rows of desks that define many traditional classrooms with cemeteries.

> As I perused the scenery, I noticed that all of the tombstones were equidistant from one another. The rows were impeccably aligned; each faced the same direction. . . . My heart sank when I thought about how this space—a cemetery—resembled the classroom space I designed for my very first class of fourth graders. The learning space I created early on as a teacher would have looked almost identical to this cemetery if drawn as a map. Add an oversized wooden desk in the corner and an interactive whiteboard and a U.S. flag on the front wall, and you have not only the first classroom environment I created but also an environment that resembles many of today's learning spaces. (Retrieved from https://www.edutopia.org/blog/rebooting-industrial-era-seating-eric-sheninger-thomas-murray?utm_source=Edutopia%20 News&utm_campaign=2406af8c02-EMAIL_CAMPAIGN_062117_enews_ rebootingindustrial_mc&utm_medium=email&utm_term=0_29295b4c8b-2406af8c02-47830463)

This comparison to what Murray and Sheninger pen "the cemetery effect" reflects the "one-size-fits-all" education model prevalent since the mid-19th century. Lately, a movement to redesign learning spaces has emerged all over the country and world. From bright colors to soft seating to flexible design, classrooms of today are beginning to resemble modern workspaces as opposed to cemeteries or factories.

STUDENT INPUT IN SCIENCE LAB REDESIGN

Bullis, Filippi, and Lubelfeld (2016) share comments about the successful science lab redesign in the Deerfield Public Schools. The 12-lab redesign, in two phases over a two-year period, reflected the efforts of a 140-person task force comprised of students, parents, teachers, administrators, board members, and members of the business community. Student voice was elevated from invisible to invaluable during this highly successful process.

> Phase one took part in the oldest and smallest of the four labs during the summer of 2014, and the remaining eight labs were completed in 2015. This provided an

opportunity for the phase two labs to be further improved by soliciting feedback from students and staff that experienced learning in the completed phase one labs.

Every square centimeter of space in the science labs and classrooms is available for learning, as defined by our current needs, but the spaces are also available for the learning of tomorrow. The labs won the Learning by Design award for "Outstanding Project" in spring 2016, as well as an "Award of Merit" for the Exhibition of Educational Environments Awards at the Joint Annual Conference of the Illinois Association of School Boards, the Illinois Association of School Administrators, and the Illinois Association of School Business Officials in 2015. Bullis, Filippi, and Lubelfeld (2016)

The old labs had fallen out of repair and clearly out of contemporary learning—not just science, but learning in general. Electricity, water, gas, and technology were in limited supply. Heavy fixed tables did not allow for movement, change, or flexibility. One thousand square feet did not allow for much more than the standard twenty-five-student class. Kids' experiences were as drab and dreary as the rooms themselves! There was nothing special, nothing engaging, and nothing fun or motivating about the spaces!

Figure 5.1 shows the original labs and hallway space with lockers, while figure 5.2 shows the completely transformed and redesigned learning spaces.

After walking into the lab represented in figure 5.2, student voice was captured on video (see https://drive.google.com/file/d/0BxY802reUAP VMmF0TkdfYm1oaDQ/view): "My first impression when I walked in was, Wait a minute, was that a robot or what is this? This is awesome; I can't wait to start using this!" The original 1961 labs shown in figure 5.1 were designed for teacher-centered instruction. The new labs shown in figure 5.2 were designed for learner-centered instruction.

Figure 5.1 1961-Era Science Lab

Figure 5.2 2017-Era Science Lab

The new labs were designed with the Next Generation Science Standards as well as learner-centered needs like mobile chairs, tables, projection devices allowing triangulation, and more. No longer did the teacher "command" the front of the room. In the new labs, the new learning spaces, there is no front of the room. Learning is messy and fluid, not stale and static. The new spaces reflect the needs of the modern learner, and student voice impacted the design.

Following the initial redesign, we captured student reflections (https://youtube/PsC751QOhgc). An example of one of these reflections is from this video: "My first impression when I walked into the lab, Wow! When I walked through the lab I thought, how are we going to use all of this technology? When I first walked into the science lab I thought it was really cool. You can look at all different screens, you can learn from every angle. This year we can do a lot of experiments, we have much more space in the labs. My first lab was a contamination lab and we got to work with the other classes (because of) moveable walls."

Student voice and input joined teacher voice and input as the first phase of labs laid the groundwork for the second phase of labs. By incorporating reactions and reflections from students, the entire learning experience and the potential future learning experience transformed and reflected the needs and wants of the students. This is significant for many reasons, engagement, morale, climate, and so forth. In addition, as Quaglia et al. (2016) discovered:

> Students who believe they have a voice in school are 7x more likely to be academically motivated than students who do not believe they have a voice. (p. 6)

Quaglia et al. (2016) take their readers through a review of the conditions they found to make an impact with respect to student voice: belonging, heroes, sense of accomplishment, fun and excitement, curiosity and creativity, spirit of adventure, leadership and responsibility, confidence to take action, and communication. Their research and findings come from more than three decades of review and study in the area of stakeholder engagement.

There are many ways to measure your district or school levels of engagement. Throughout this book, we are sharing "ASK'EM" ideas and examples

Figure 5.3 Belonging Measure

from practice. Also Quaglia has many resources. In addition, in figure 5.3 one of the school's results in the domain of belonging are shown. In Mike's district, they measure student engagement annually through a survey instrument for students in grades three to eight as well as follow-up action planning.

THE NEW LIBRARY-LEARNING COMMONS

> I walk into almost all of our schools in West Vancouver and very often the first thing people want to show me or talk to me about is the changes happening around the library. Or more specifically, schools are taking great pride in their learning commons spaces that are developing. While the physical spaces are exciting, the changes to our mindsets are far more powerful. We are not destined for new schools in West Vancouver anytime soon but the rethink of the library has been both a symbolic and concrete shift in how we think about space and how we think about learning. The school library – a centre piece in schools – is now the modern hub for learning.
>
> Retrieved from: https://cultureofyes.ca/2015/02/12/the-learning-commons-mindset/

Visitors to Deerfield Public Schools District 109 in the 2016–2017 school year saw more than world-class science classrooms and laboratories at the middle schools. They also had an opportunity to see the reimagined elementary library learning commons instructional spaces, which were renovated during the summer of 2016.

The libraries include some traditional materials while also incorporating SMART Labs for hands-on STEAM experiences and multimedia project creation. In Deerfield, they believe that the library serves as a hub for learning with an emphasis on the 4Cs of 21st-century learning, communication, collaboration, critical thinking, and creativity. These newly designed spaces engage, inspire, and empower all students to become active participants in their learning experience.

> "Shush!" is a sound librarians do not want children to hear anymore when they enter the library in *Deerfield* Public Schools District 109. The district is spending $2 million to prove the point. The libraries will be equipped with STEM

(science, technology, engineering and math) and creative media arts (CMA) features as well as new furniture—all designed to help students collaborate with each other. That means there will be a lot more talking in the library, according to Marcie Faust, the district's director of innovative learning.

Faust said the changes are being made with the four basic tenets of 21st Century education in mind—communication, collaboration, critical thinking and creativity. "The first two can't happen in silence," Faust said. "Now kids have to communicate. If the library is a quiet zone, all of that won't be possible." When the project is done, the role of the library will be very different from what it is now, according to Kipling Principal Anthony McConnell. He said it will no longer be just a repository for books to borrow.

(Retrieved from http://www.chicagotribune.com/suburbs/deerfield/news/ct-dfr-d109-libraries-tl-1210-20151207-story.html)

The library should be the learning hub for the school. For this to become real, students must want to be in the library. There needs to be books for all types of student interests, and there needs to be comfortable and flexible seating. Today's students are used to comfort, they are used to sitting on the floor, lying on the rug, hanging out on the couch. The realization that school spaces are for students becomes the imperative mind-set when elevating student voice from invisible to invaluable.

Some of the teachers at Alan B. Shepard Middle School in Deerfield challenged the students to give input on the new library learning commons. Sarah Guillen (social studies), Becca Frase (math), Andrea Trudeau (library information specialist), Alex Rummelhart and Sarah Ball (English language arts [ELA]), and others engaged, inspired, and empowered their students! The project assignment is spelled out in table 5.1, and student blueprints are featured starting with figure 5.4.

Table 5.1 Text from Informational Presentation of Design Project

Project description
Be an Innovator!
Sixth Grade Shepard Middle School
Andrea Trudeau
Rebecca Frase
Sarah Guillen
Key Knowledge, Understanding, and Success Skills
Application of interdisciplinary skills:
I can solve real-world and mathematical problems involving area, surface area, and volume. (CCSS.MATH.CONTENT.6.G.A.1)
I can write essential questions to help me figure out the best design for the LC. (SS. IS.1.6–8)

(Continued)

Table 5.1 (Continued)

I can create a design that considers the impact on people and environment. (MS-ETS1–1)

I can write informative/explanatory texts to examine a topic and convey ideas, concepts, and information through the selection, organization, and analysis of relevant content. (ELACC6W2)

I can present arguments and explanations that would appeal to audiences and venues outside the classroom using a variety of media (SS.IS.6.6–8.MC)

AND demonstration of Habits of Success:

I can collaborate with others.

I can demonstrate innovative thinking in order to solve a problem.

Challenging Problem or Question

How can WE redesign the Shepard Learning Commons to reflect our innovative spirit and creativity?

Sustained Inquiry

Inquiry Standards from Sixth-Grade Social Studies Illinois State Standards

Create essential questions.

Construct explanations using a variety of media.

Authenticity

Learning Commons is slated for renovation in the summer of 2018.

We are looking to incorporate student input in this redesign.

Panel will include stakeholders and experts who will also have input in the redesign.

Architects and interior designers will help to frontload information.

Student Voice and Choice

Students' design options are completely open-ended; the sky is the limit!

Small product (blueprint or small scale model)

Final presentation format choice

Reflection

Informal journal reflections

Exit slips

Reflection opportunities will be almost daily and at the conclusion of the project.

Critique and Revision

Feedback in different formats

Q&A with experts

Charrette with peers

Gallery walk (backward post-its)

Group conferences with teacher

Multiple opportunities to create drafts

Appointments available with stakeholders

Final innovation/collaboration rubric will have written feedback from teachers.

Public product

Student groups will create a small-scale model or blueprint, a written proposal, and a final presentation that includes a sales pitch to key stakeholders and experts.

Student products will be shared via social media: Twitter, Periscope, and Facebook.

Elements from student designs will influence Learning Commons redesign in 2018.

Figure 5.4 Student Design Blueprint

Each subject area then took a focus for assessment and guidance during the project's course. For example, math was responsible for measurements and diagrams, science for modeling, and so on.

The English teachers helped craft and guide tools for improving the student presentation and voice piece, helping them assess their speaking and listening skills on an ELA rubric, and generally guiding them in making their pitches during a share fair activity.

So everyone on every team was involved with all aspects of the project (which made this a great experience for all sixth graders and teachers). Each subject area and teacher also were responsible for helping groups succeed with tools and instruction that they could use within their groups to excel.

COMMON AREAS

In addition to libraries, there are many other nonclassroom learning spaces that can come alive in school. At Wilmot Elementary School in Deerfield, students provided their input as to the types of furniture they wanted to see placed in the library. They also had a great deal to do with a common area renovation and upgrade.

Principal Eileen Brett met with student groups frequently to gain their insight for the types of furniture and colors they wanted in that commons area. Mrs. Lathan, the library information specialist, also participated in those meetings.

At the middle school level, the principals asked for student input into hallway areas, space under stairways, and entryways. In the middle schools where space was once barren, with student input, comfortable and inviting seating now exists. Simply by asking students (ASK'EM), the feel and design of the school changed profoundly. Now there are couches, seats, tables, and inviting spaces that make learning available everywhere. With student input and creative leadership, hallways and other common areas become learning spaces.

ASK'EM

Ask: Ask the users, students, teachers, support staff, and so on what they think about the physical design of the learning spaces. Ask when the last renovations or redesign took place. Ask what the capital plans are for upgrades and redesign. Ask a local designer or architect to lead a visioning process with stakeholders.

Support: Support the needs of all learners with personalized furniture and options. For example, for kids who fidget, put Velcro under all desks and tables so anyone who needs that type of sensory input can get it. Normalize the needs that children have.

Know: Know the latest trends in design thinking and work space changes in the "real world." For example, check out a renovated public library, and imagine that type of environment in your learning spaces.

Empower: Empower others to act. That is one of the five exemplary practices of a leader (Kouzes & Posner, 2007). Empower students to have a voice in design of learning spaces, common areas, the grounds, and any other major projects. Empower teachers to work with architects and designers so that the user experience is considered in any change or redesign efforts.

Monitor: Monitor the impact of the physical design through surveys and focus groups. Check student engagement, student learning, teacher morale, and maintenance cleaning input. Check on all of the elements of the design. What did your design changes intend to measure? Think about these topics in advance so you know what you are looking for.

SUMMARY

Schools used to resemble prisons, factories, and hospitals; now they resemble modern learning, or do they? They can and they should. Progressive educators seem to agree that the industrial model of seating and school design no longer best serves the needs of our students. Using the voice of the student, as discussed in this chapter, explore how to best leverage existing and traditional learning spaces in addition to exploring what schools of the future should look like.

Gone are the days where learning was permitted only in classrooms or designated areas. Now the bright colors, soft seating, couches, moveable tables, and other workplace furniture transform hallways into learning spaces. The library is no longer a "shush" place. Students want to be valued and engaged in the learning process. Learning is far more than classroom coursework. Learning embodies student voice in the design process, and this gives students pride and ownership in the overall experience of school.

In chapter 6, we look at student voice in communications and public relations (PR). Who better than students to share what really matters and what is really going on in school? If they don't tell their stories, someone else will! Another example from the field about student input into the design of schools can be accessed here: https://youtu.be/UHX53qAo4b0.

Student Voice in District Communication—PR Branding

Inside each of us is a natural born storyteller just waiting to be released.

—Robin Moore

Our Main Customers Are Students, Let Them Tell Our Story
Storyteller in Chief
Challenges of Branding Your School
Power of Social Media
Extension of Curriculum: Examples from the field
Takeaways, Lessons Learned, and Next Steps
Summary
Guest Commentary from Student Dariusz Warzocha

Reflection Questions

If you asked a student, teacher, or parent what the "story" of your school was, how many of them would tell the same story as you?

Who do you think your community would rather hear from to know the story of your school, the kids, or from you?

What is the primary fear keeping you (teacher, principal, superintendent) from handing over communication duties to students?

Who, within your organization, has the most knowledge of social media and social media trends? How are you including them in the conversation of how to brand your school?

Stop-Think-Act

Stop: All districts, schools, and classrooms have a communications plan with important stakeholders whether formally documented or one that occurs naturally in day-to-day practice.

Think: Students are capable communicators, engagers, and incredible navi-
gators of electronic platforms (the medium of the day), yet we often do
not include them in this process and almost never allow them ownership
of this process.

Act: Today, give one key communication process to students, not simply to
do but to own. It just might accomplish the goals of communication better
than the current program.

OUR MAIN CUSTOMERS ARE STUDENTS,
LET THEM TELL OUR STORY

There is no shortage of talent competitions on television. One of the best
parts of these shows is always the try-out stage. There is something compelling about trying to figure out which act will be a success based on the very
dramatic buildup presented for each contestant. In a recent episode of one
such television show, a little nine-year-old girl by the name of Angela Hale
was introduced to America.

Her story was fantastic (a kidney transplant survivor), and she was ador-
able and full of energy. She was incredibly easy to root for. The time came for
her to demonstrate her talent, and when she began to sing, the nine-year-old
girl with a squeaky voice transformed before the nation's eyes and sounded
like an angel. Goosebumps first. Tears second.

George Couros is a leading speaker and author in education. He has a tremendous message and is a great thinker. His ability to present and communicate with an audience supersedes both of those previous gifts, however. George
has the unique ability to seamlessly integrate video into his presentation.

Through video, it seems that not only is he delivering the message, but
more importantly, the videos he uses almost universally rely on children
delivering the message and therefore delivering his message. George gets
it. As skilled an orator as he may be, he knows that the authentic voice of
children will always be the best communicator when it comes to education.

Mikaela Ulmer's new product landed a coveted spot on the shelf at Whole
Foods. In doing so, this nine-year-old from Texas beat out massive conglomer-
ates such as Kraft, Pepsi, and many others. Her product, Bee Sweet Lemonade,
is not only a fantastic product born out of a fantastic purpose of helping restore
the alarmingly rapid drop in bee population but also was created after a series of
events originally constructed as a stimulus to help her overcome her own fear of
bees.

Not only is she an entrepreneur—she is a salesperson too. When asked why
she thought her product made it to the shelves at Whole Foods and why she

received a lucrative contract to make her product when competitors did not, she simply answered, "I do not know. Do they make theirs with love?"

These examples are pertinent for two reasons. First, kids are incredibly compelling and easier to root for than adult counterparts. Second, the "story" matters. Talent or a great message has less appeal than the same output with a compelling backstory.

This has everything to do with what we do wrong when branding our schools and districts. When any person with heart heard Angela Hale sing, it meant more to hear her be successful than it would have if she were twenty-five years old. When George masterfully weaves together a presentation using student video, it brings emotion and kindness to a presentation that addresses some dramatically uncomfortable truths about the state of education.

When you read about Mikaela's genius, innovation, and salesmanship, it compels you more to act than a story of a successful entrepreneur who is thirty-nine years old and sells products at Whole Foods.

The simple truth is that kids are engaging in a manner that adults can only hope to be. Kids present as authentic, real, vulnerable, and more than capable communicators. Kids inspire empathy. Kids are given the benefit of the doubt. The average person wants the average kid to succeed, and this causes them to consume the information differently.

Compare this against what we typically see in how schools brand themselves. Essentially, we have "suits" spouting facts in an effort to attempt to engage our communities. There is no story—there is no context. This is our practice when we have a resource at our fingertips that is free, engaging, and more than capable.

Who do you think your community would rather hear from to know the story of your school, the kids or you? Who do you think can better provide context explaining why your classroom, school, or district is phenomenal? Still, however, most schools seldom use this invaluable resource that is eminently available and continue upon traditional methodologies from branding ourselves despite little to no evidence of any success.

STORYTELLER IN CHIEF

The ability to make up, communicate, and consume stories is essentially what makes us human. On the TED stage, Yuval Noah Harari explains this concept brilliantly. While we encourage all of you to listen to this talk, we will do our best to synthesize his speech in a few short sentences. The ability to imagine the future, think of things bigger and better than they currently are, and to conceptualize religion and faith is an essential part of what makes us uniquely human.

Think about this, would a chimpanzee ever not do something its instincts instruct it to do because it is worried about how it will impact its ability to launch a startup it has thought up in a few months? Of course not, and while that is a dramatic oversimplification of the concept, we trust you get the point. Storytelling is, in essence, part of our DNA.

For decades, the stories of our schools have been created by our communities and have become the narrative defining our institutions. In some areas, this has been done very intentionally, and in others, the narrative has been allowed to write itself. In some areas, "our story" has been crafted by the leadership of a school or district, and in other places, the narrative has been written by the community due to the void in communication provided by leadership.

In 2014, author, speaker, and educational thought leader Eric Sheninger transformed a term that had been tossed around about President Barack Obama on social media and blog platforms—*storyteller-in-chief*. Sheninger used this term to challenge school leaders to assume that role for their buildings. Eric demanded school leaders understand the importance of discussing the "story" of our schools in the ever-changing information age.

CHALLENGES OF BRANDING YOUR SCHOOL

Challenge 1: What Is Your Story?

The number one challenge in branding your school in any capacity is understanding what story you want to tell. This may be hard to understand in the context of school, so we will use college recruiting as an example. If you were one of the top high school football players in the country in December 2012, it is easy to understand why you may have wanted to attend the University of Alabama, the University of Southern California, or Ohio State University.

It is less apparent why you might give other (traditionally) less successful schools like Western Michigan the time of day. Programs in that situation must develop a narrative about what they are doing and make it compelling enough for seventeen- and eighteen-year-olds to decide to join that movement. Great recruiters and head coaches, like PJ Fleck, are able to do this. This is why the elite schools occasionally have new competition in that elite realm from time to time, and why schools like Western Michigan make it to a Bowl Championship Series game like they did in 2016.

The challenge is knowing your story and being able to tell it. PJ was able to, in his first year, secure the top recruiting class in his conference despite the woeful performance of his team prior to his arrival. PJ was able to tell his story in a way that was different. All recruiters and all schools generally look the same on the outside. They all have the same purpose. Figuring out what your school or district believes in, values, and demonstrates as a core competency is the first step to being able to tell your unique story.

Is your school at the cutting edge of innovation, or is it doing the best it can with limited resources to stay competitive in an ever-changing world? Are you implementing a program such as Leader in Me and the full commitment of your school is to developing everyone's unique genius? All three are compelling story lines, and there are a million more potential narratives defining our schools right now. We just have to decode them and package them for our students and our community.

PJ was able to tell a story of unity, purpose, love, and hard work that set his program apart. "Row the boat" became the rallying cry of the program well before the work led to demonstrable success. It was only after a compelling story could be told that success followed.

Challenge 2—Who Is Telling Your Story?

We cannot cogently answer question number two until we have an answer to question number one. It is impossible to truly tell your story without knowing what it is. Regardless of whether you are intentionally telling your story or not, however, as teachers, principals, and district administrators, we must realize we are constantly telling our story. Whether or not we are intentionally telling the narrative of what is happening in our schools or not, we are communicating something to people.

Think about that and consider how communication typically looks. Are we reactionary and responsive all the time? Do we only tell the good stuff and appear disingenuous? Do we focus on the parts of the job we find important like finance or a pet program and ignore other key aspects of schooling?

The point is, like it or not, there is a narrative about your school being told. So you need to figure out what your number one customer (the students) and other key stakeholders believe that story is and whether or not it is accurate. More importantly, we need to figure out who is telling the story that the people are truly listening to.

PJ Fleck, his staff, and his team decided to own this message. Row the Boat became a national phenomenon as this effort, this phrase, and the slowly changing outcomes defined an entire program. This was not just PJ. This became the story the entire team told. This is key, because as the adults and educators in the room, we believe you will be shocked at how much influence students and parents already have in communicating your message without any intentionality on the part of the school.

Challenge 3—Is the Current Story the Story You Want?

In almost all cases, unless a teacher, principal, or other administrator has very intentionally tried to create a narrative around their school or district, the current story of the school is probably not the most desired description. This does not mean that all schools have a negative reputation.

This may mean that a school is very academically successful but has a great football team, and the public narrative is that the school is "sports first." Or a school is working extremely hard on personalized learning and competency-based reporting, and the narrative is that there are great people in the school, but they are trying too hard to be something that does not reflect this community.

As a result, the first job of any educator reading this chapter is to figure out what the story is for your classroom, building, or district and have an obscenely direct conversation with yourself on whether or not that story is satisfactory. If it is not, as leaders, we must change our behaviors in order to inspire different results. All systems are perfectly designed to produce current results—if we want different results, we must first change the system.

Challenge 4—If the Story Is Not What You Want, How Do You Change the Narrative?

This may seem like the hardest question, but this is where it gets easy. If we want to change the narrative, we engage in a very real conversation with students. Remember, there is our truth or there is the story we tell. There is their truth or the story they believe as true, and then there is the objective truth. If we want to change the narrative of our school, we have to work with our kids to ensure that the story we *want* to tell is the experience they are currently living. If not, we are simply telling a fictitious story to both ourselves and the public.

Challenge 5—If the Story Is What We Want to Share, How Do We Amplify the Message?

Again, this is easy. Give this away to our students. If we want a message spread about our schools, there is no greater conduit to the general public than our students. Moreover, there is no greater way to impact students than to have other students spread the message. Changing and amplifying the narrative of your classroom, school, or district may seem like tough work, and it is.

The essential part to remember, however, is that once the message begins to change, communication takes place at an exponential rate. Think of it as a flywheel. It may take a while to get moving, but once it does, the momentum provided allows for continued progress to be much easier than gaining initial movement.

To continue the dive into PJ Fleck as a leader, a communicator, and a wonderful storyteller, his work to change the narrative around his football program started with him. PJ was obsessed with not allowing average work to define him or his team. He was determined to force his team to see the sum as being greater than the parts and that their duty was to give their absolute best every day. He lived this. He talked this. He imparted this upon his team until they carried the message for him.

Coach Fleck points to Corey Davis often as the modicum of why the story of row the boat is so important. Corey, the number five pick in the 2017 NFL draft who was not offered a scholarship by any other Division One football program, and a nationally recognized star, says this about the "story" he was told as a Western Michigan football player: "I kind of wish I knew 'Row the Boat' when I was a little kid. Whatever adversity you're facing, just keep pushing, keep going through it. You can't control the past, you can only learn from it."

How?

It is very possible that this all sounds well and good, but branding your classroom, school, or district is something you had never thought about previously. The "challenge" of giving this work away to students might not seem that difficult, but the actual question of how to brand a school or lead this process may be sticking out as the main question in your head right now. Do not worry!

This is perfectly natural. One (great) characteristic of most educators is their humility. Most of us went into this profession for the right reason—to serve kids. With that end in mind, press relations and marketing are not something that come naturally to many of us. There is help, however.

The help, primarily, is already within you. Everyone who has read a leadership or self-help book of any kind has some semblance of an idea of how to create a plan. One template we prefer to follow is simple and outlined in table 6.1.

An example of a "completed" goal template is found in table 6.2 so that it is easier to visualize what this may actually look like. This plan is not complex or complete but is intended to be illustrative of how simple the template can be used to help guide a plan.

The question may still be looming—how do I do this? The answer is simple. Have a vision and then involve others. One of the subthemes of this entire book is liberation. As a teacher, principal, or superintendent, you are not responsible for having every good idea or carrying out every successful initiative. The same is true here.

Table 6.1 Parent Goal Template

Smart Goal
Activities to Achieve Goal
Timeline
Responsible Person/People
Deliverable to Be Produced at This Stage

The table can be expanded to include as many activities or action steps as necessary to achieve the goal.

Table 6.2 Parent Goal (completed example)

Parent Goal: Increase the School's Digital Footprint

Smart Goal: Increase twitter followers and Facebook likes by 20 percent in the next quarter	Activities to Achieve Goal	Timeline	Responsible Person/People	Deliverable to Be Produced at This Stage
	Parent e-mail home	Immediate	Student advisory group to write e-mail, to be delivered by district office secretary	Physical copy of the e-mail
	Student assembly	Sept. 20˅	Selected students from each building	Copy of the consistent PowerPoint to be shared
	Student to student promotion	Oct. 2	Individual student advisory councils	Copy of the schedule for students to address individual classrooms
	Creation of local hashtag (#) to increase	Nov. 1	Principals oversee district-wide vote	Google Forms results page

If your classroom, building, or school does not have a brand and you want to create one, then create action and involve others. That is your fundamental responsibility. Having a cogent and inspiring plan is not yours to own. It is the collective brilliance of those you work with and serve that will create this.

Still stuck? There are professional organizations, for instance, NSPRA (National School Public Relations Association), which do a wonderful job of providing resources and also highlighting great work. Additionally, NSPRA has thirty-three local chapters, so many states have their own localized version where like-minded school professionals can work together to create incredible ideas to promote their classroom, school, or district *and* the incredible work taking place in all schools.

POWER OF SOCIAL MEDIA

If you are still doubting social media, stop! If you are still doubting the power of social media in schools, stop! If our imploring you to stop is not enough, let us share a story with you about PJ Caposey's father.

From PJ:

Let me start by saying my father is my hero. He was not an academic. He was not one to speak unnecessarily. He was not without flaws. But, he worked. And he worked. And he worked. He showed me that whatever life I wanted to create for myself and my family was possible, but there were no shortcuts. More importantly, he never complained. Five, 16-hour shifts in a row only leaving work to coach my baseball team, and then return back to work—no complaints.

And then—it was the last 1990s and I was in high school. My father was seated at our dinner table. Shirt off (customary), gold chain with Italian horn swinging, and a gallon jug of iced tea as a drink sitting in front of him and he started to complain. The new boss was demanding that all employees start using this new thing called email immediately. He was furious. He blamed the boss, complained about the needless change, and then defended his position vehemently. Why would we need email when we have interoffice tube mail and fax machines? This was outrageous!!

This sounds absurd now, but was not an abnormal reaction then. Today, my father emails. He still uses all caps all the time, but that is a different battle to fight on a different day. The point is, he made it there. Everyone made it there. He bet against email—was forced into compliance—and now he is an active emailer. Email, which was once a novel and commonly resisted idea, is now here and is never going away. There were hundreds of thousands of people like my father that saw email as one more thing that would never become a ubiquitous part of our society.

The point is that e-mail of the 1990s is social media of today. Social media is big business. Remember when people thought Snapchat would certainly fail. Snapchat's valuation was $24 billion in the first quarter of 2017. Do not be PJ's father and resist change because you are comfortable. Do not be PJ's father and resist because you are intentionally not seeing the benefits and the power of a new tool. Most importantly, do not resist because you do not know enough about social media and you simply do not have the time to be an expert on one more thing.

We work in schools and there are no greater experts in social media than our students. The beauty and the complexity of social media is that the platforms change so frequently and without a great deal of public notice for some time. For instance, as this book is being written, most junior high principals and classroom teachers (unless they have kids of the same age) have no idea what musical.ly is or how it works. This app has been the leading free download via iOS in nineteen different countries!

The point of this is not for you to go out and learn a ton about musical.ly. The point is that by the time you are reading this book, there may be one, two, or seven new apps that take its place. The rise, fall, and "stickiness" of social media sites are relatively unpredictable, and the volatility is tremendous. This is precisely why school leaders must work with their students and rely on them to be the experts of the arena and trust them implicitly to lead them down the appropriate road.

EXTENSION OF CURRICULUM: EXAMPLES FROM THE FIELD

If a goal (whether stated or implicit) of a school is not to produce citizens with an exceptionally positive digital footprint given they are entering a world largely dominated by technology, we are doing our kids a disservice. Learning how to communicate, leverage markets, build reputation and image, and connect with others via social medium is the coin of our realm.

Schools choosing to "block" and ignore social media because it is easier for the adults are doing a fundamental disservice to the kids we are serving. Does social media present a fair level of risk? Yes—absolutely. So does driving a vehicle, but we teach driver's education, for example, in schools. We must overcome our fear and make decisions based on what is best for kids—not what we feel is best for us as adults. (Recall chapter 3 and the extensive attention to digital citizenship.)

Gladstone High

Gladstone High responded to cyberbullying with a positive social media campaign to demonstrate the great things that high school students are capable of and that the good in their school outweighed the bad. A few, simple thematic days made a dramatic difference.

A couple of the unique themes that students came up with included "Sweet Tweet Tuesday" for students to deliver compliments to others via the online platform. Another day was "Whatcha Know Wednesday" where students were encouraged to take a selfie with someone they did not know well and post an interesting fact about that person.

Hinkley-Big Rock

The district has a unified blog that sends out important information throughout the course of the year. This in and of itself is a great step in branding your district and creating a more meaningful connection with stakeholders. Hinkley-Big Rock took it one step further, however. They actively recruit and include student bloggers to tell the real story of what is taking place in their district. This not only empowers the student writing but also excites the community and gives them a true glimpse into what students think of the school they are supporting.

Oregon High School

While this is not an example of students leveraging their talents to create great PR for their school, it is an example of student wisdom and to provide confidence in handing school PR over to students. Yik Yak, a dangerous (and now-defunct) social media platform, invaded the school and began to create a negative and hostile atmosphere.

Yik Yak would allow people to post anonymously, and the bullying was reaching a fever pitch—particularly among the ninth-grade students. As these issues continued to emerge, the district called together a leadership team meeting to create a plan to address the situation. Counselor interventions, assemblies, and new consequence guidelines were established at the emergency meeting.

The next morning came, and the buzz around Yik Yak was entirely gone. It ended when respected and influential twelfth-grade students expressed to their high school classmates that what was going on was not cool and was not okay in their school. Yik Yak essentially died in Oregon High School that day. The moral of the story is that the majority of kids know right and wrong, want to do the right thing, and can powerfully lead their peers if, and only if, (sometimes) the adults get out of their way.

TAKEAWAYS, LESSONS LEARNED, AND NEXT STEPS

Leadership in PR and branding is as simple as being able to ask the question what is our story and how do we tell it. One person cannot effectively "own" the responsibility of being the district's "storyteller." Students have better knowledge and insight into where the majority of students and parents are connecting online and how than most education professionals do.

Allowing students to become more involved in PR efforts not only offloads work from teachers and administrators, but it actually teaches valuable lessons that students can continue to employ after their schooling ends. Fear is what prevents leaders from taking logical next steps forward. There is nothing to fear about giving students additional responsibility to tell the story of the district.

Throughout the entirety of this book, the acronym, ASK'EM, has been employed as a framework or methodology to use in order to best engage your students in a process and leverage their unique voice. Below is a quick outline of how to start engaging your students in this process.

Ask—Ask your students what they think the "story" of your classroom, school, or district currently is and what they would like it to be. The term *story* as it relates to school communications is a bit nebulous. Substituting the word *image* for *story* or changing the phrasing entirely is appropriate to ensure that students are expressing what it really means to be a student and what they wish it really meant to be a student.

Support—Speaking on behalf of anyone other than yourself takes courage and can be quite intimidating. For students to feel comfortable telling the story of your school, it is going to take love, support, and time from the adults nurturing students along this transformation. Remember, the best support you can give students is the steadfast permission to always tell the truth. Student communication on behalf of the school should not be about spin. It should be a true, authentic narrative.

Know—It is important to know the strengths of your students. As mentioned earlier in this chapter, social media is a resounding strength our students have. Leverage this unique and emerging skill to better communicate for your community.

Empower—Any broadcaster can read a teleprompter. A great newsman or newswoman helps take the news of the day and creates stories that are interesting to the consumer. The same must hold true when we allow students to take the lead on PR for our schools. Students must be empowered to tell a story about what life as a student really looks like and hold that against the standard of what school environment is trying to be created.

Monitor—While I am the fiercest proponent for student ownership and accountability, every successful venture must have accountability. This does not mean censorship, but it means that messages being conveyed on behalf of the school have a level of professionalism and dignity (this also extends to how a transition such as this has such merit as a subcomponent of curriculum based in communications, marketing, etc.). Additionally, effort without goals and desired outcomes means little. This process should drive toward some desired and measurable outcome.

SUMMARY

PR and branding have quickly become embedded in the job descriptions of school leaders. Some are embracing this, and some are stuck frozen without any confidence in moving forward. This is where our brilliant students come forward with a natural solution.

Our students are capable communicators, tech savvy, and social media savants and can tell the true story of your school better than any scripted message you can write. This chapter helps guide the adults in the building through the process of letting go and ceding control when it comes to communication so that students can lead the way and grow their experiences and resumes in the process.

GUEST COMMENTARY FROM HIGH SCHOOL STUDENT DARIUSZ WARZOCHA

I initially reached out to the Meridian CUSD 223 School District on February 1, 2015 through the District's Facebook page and asked for, whoever it was who read the messages, to take a look at a video project that I have been working on for several months. This video project focused on my father, who is a long-life, over-the-road truck driver, and his journeys throughout the United States of America.

These little projects were uploaded to YouTube, where I hoped they would gain some exposure. In my message to the district, I asked if one of these projects could be shared as a student's work in the district. I had absolutely no idea what to expect after pressing the send button—my parents, in fact, told me to think before sending the message because maybe my message was something that might not have been viewed as "professional" or that could "waste other people's time."

Nevertheless, I took the chance and I hit send. Two hours later I received a response from Mr. Caposey (at the time), asking to meet me face-to-face, as he found my project very interesting. What occurred at that meeting, most definitely, changed my life. When I met with Mr. Caposey, for the first time, he asked me how I got started doing these video projects, how long I have been working on them, and other interesting questions about my passion.

He continued to state that he sees a fantastic opportunity for me. Then, he proposed the idea of me completing some video production work for the district, and in exchange for my time and work, I would be given the equipment that I would find necessary to complete the work. At the time, I was a freshman in high School, working with a camera that was falling apart—far from professional.

After a day or two of considering Mr. Caposey's offer, I accepted it as I knew that this was an opportunity that I knew I could grow from. Furthermore, this opportunity would provide me with the equipment I would need to further follow my passion. A dream of mine was to be able to have my own equipment, and go produce wedding films, business commercials, and any other projects that I could possibly get involved with.

At the time, and even today, the current limiting factor to my passion was money! Video cameras themselves are expensive, and professional video cameras and equipment is even more expensive! I knew that with the right equipment, I would be able to create incredible quality products. Accepting Mr. Caposey's offer turned into a "no brainer."

Mr. Caposey's first idea for me was to start creating monthly "recap" videos about the Board of Education's agenda and meetings. This was an effort to try to increase transparency and communication between the district and the community through technology. Along with these monthly videos, I was tasked with creating the district YouTube channel to expand the district's social media and online presence.

I was given tasks to complete, like the monthly videos or the YouTube channel; however, the way I chose to go about completing the tasks was always entirely up to me. I always had full creative direction on where I wanted to go with all projects, and I believe it was because of this that I could grow and further advance my skills. We continued with these monthly videos for about a year or so before Mr. Caposey approached me with a personal project for him.

He asked if he could get a personal video completed for an application which he was submitting. He made it clear that this was something separate from my typical district video production work, and because of that he told me he was more than willing to pay for the work. Dr. Caposey did not stop there.

In the spring of 2016, Dr. Caposey nominated me for the Illinois Chapter/National School Public Relations Association Distinguished Service Award of Excellence. On May 12, 2016 I went to Bolingbrook, Illinois with Dr. Caposey and other district staff members to receive my award. Of course, Dr. Caposey and the other staff members present were also being recognized for their own accomplishments. I was one of two students in the state to receive the award for "Enhancing the understanding and support of public education, thereby benefiting our schools, students and communities."

Between the work I was doing for this district and Dr. Caposey, I didn't have any real and regular "clients." It was Dr. Caposey and John Smith, the Board of Education President, who introduced me to the director of the Burpee Museum in Rockford. Soon enough, I was doing regular video production work for the Burpee Museum and for the exhibits inside. I finally had my first regular client. It did not stop there!

More and more opportunities soon became available to me, such as me working on larger and more difficult projects for the district such as filming the graduation ceremony at the high school with multiple cameras, and then producing what I captured into a final film that would be burned onto over a hundred DVD's and become available for sale.

After some time, Dr. Caposey approached me with the idea of having video production become one of my classes at the high school. An "independent study" he called it. Instead of going to a class, I would work on video production work. Specifically, one project—to create a promotional video for each building in the school district. A total of four videos, with interviews from staff members and students was a huge undertaking.

From initially contacting the principals of each building, to scheduling meetings and film dates with the staff members, to the actual filming and editing of the projects, this was the biggest learning experience, in regard to video production, in my life. Soon my work grew from just video production, into photography and website design. Dr. Caposey approached me, asking for me to build him a new website as his current one was severely outdated.

I never said no to any project, even when I knew I had no idea how to do certain things, as I was more than willing to learn just so that I could take the fullest advantage of each opportunity. In this case, it was creating a blog-style website with various features that Dr. Caposey requested. Around this time Dr. Caposey also introduced me to another individual in the community, Matt Bouback.

Matt Bouback is the owner of a gym in the neighboring town and was in search of someone to do video production work for his gym. I sat down and met with Dr. Caposey and Matt one day in Dr. Caposey's office. I was a nervous wreck, even though I probably (hopefully) did not show it; however, my hand was definitely shaking and there was a slight jitter in my voice. I knew that this was a huge opportunity for me, as this was someone in the local region which was looking for a service who I offered. For me, that was huge.

Today, as an incoming senior to Stillman Valley High School, I practically run my own business. Matt Bouback is one of my most regular clients, I continue to do work for the Meridian school district, and have had gained many new clients and contacts along the way. I am currently working on a website for the local fire protection district, editing and finalizing two wedding films, and am in the process of scheduling two projects with a first-time client.

I have grown from this high school freshman looking for exposure for a little video project I did, to this mature, experienced individual taking on multiple video productions at a time. I have grown from doing little videos to massive multiple camera productions, being trusted in filming other people's "once-in-a-lifetime" moments, creating websites and commercials for businesses, and even graphic design for logos and various t-shirts and other branding merchandise.

Back in May, Dr. Caposey introduced a new idea to me. Starting in August, as an "independent study," I will be managing public relations for the Meridian CUSD 223 school district through the aid of social media in pursuit of pushing and promoting #WeAreMCUSD to the community and beyond. Dr. Caposey had also made it clear, that he is more than willing to vouch for my experience if I chose to put down the work I have completed for the district onto a C/V or resume.

If Dr. Caposey had not asked me to meet him face-to-face because he saw a glimmer of talent in me, my life would be very, very different right now. The sole fact that the district has an established Facebook page made it possible for me to connect with Dr. Caposey, proving just how crucial social media is in connecting to the community. I feel that once I graduate high school, I can go out and work for myself or go out and find a job with the skillsets that I have acquired.

I feel confident that through the opportunities that Dr. Caposey has provided me with, I can graduate high school, and be prepared for the real world. The lesson here is that Dr. Caposey listened and read my initial message, and he looked out and looked ahead to try and provide me with the best possible opportunities. And for that, I will forever be grateful. Listening to students and what they have to say is crucial, because you never know what kind of talents may be lurking being their words.

Chapter 7

Personalized Learning

You can choose courage or you can choose comfort, but you cannot have both.

—Brené Brown

Why Engaged Learning?
Why Meet Individual Learner Needs?
Whose Learning Is It Anyway?
What Do Students Think?
Summary
Guest Commentary from Dr. Anthony McConnell, Assistant Superintendent for Teaching, Learning & Innovation in the Deerfield Public Schools District 109 in Deerfield, Illinois

Reflection Questions

In what ways are your teachers implementing personalized learning structures? If not, do you have plans to do so?

How are you forming a shared understanding of concepts like learner-centered and personalized learning in your organization?

How will students be involved in the transformation from adult/teacher-centered to student-centered teaching and learning?

Stop-Think-Act

Stop: How do you currently elicit student input in decision making around instructional practices or methodologies?

Think: Have you asked students what they think about the latest instructional planning around what personalized learning means?

Act: Do a deep dive into who is implementing personalized learning structures and curriculum and discover how students have been engaged in the
decision making.

WHY ENGAGED LEARNING?

Historically, the essential elements of schooling and subject/content sequence
came from a decision of the Committee of Ten from the 1890s. With these
archaic and group-focused systems and structures in place, it's proven quite
difficult to genuinely engage students in their learning at a large-scale level.
As we've referenced throughout the book, the global economy and society
have changed. Now for education, it's time for our structural changes to
reflect modern and future needs.

It is possible to change some assumptions we currently have (like Sir Ken
Robinson writes about and discusses in his popular "2010 TED Talk Changing Educational Paradigms"). He raises many relevant questions like:

• Why do we group students by age and move them through in batches?
• Why do we wait for students to fail and then offer remediation?
• Why do we hold time as the constant and learning as the variable?
• Why do we advance students based on credits and time served?

We need a system that is much more granular in terms of better calibration
to give kids feedback about what they are learning. Like the end-of-chapter
feature ASK'EM, take the time to ask a student what concepts he or she has
mastered. We need innovation and transformation, not invention or reform.
Student voice can help us shift from compliance to engagement and needed
transformation.

In our professional lives and in preparation for the writing of this book,
each of us conducted an extensive review of literature and research from
experts in the field like Bloom, Marzano, Waters, and Hattie. Their expertise
combined with our hands on leadership experiences meld together to create opportunities for action research, implementation of ideas and concepts,
and the validation of relative success in many of our change management
activities.

At a professional conference, Mike was reminded of some deeply relevant
and comprehensive studies conducted by Apple, including their 1985–1997
longitudinal study of the "why" in terms of using technology tools to amplify
and expand student learning opportunities and teacher pedagogical opportunities. In brief, as the speaker shared, the study found that engaged learners
supported by great teachers learn more than disengaged learners with not so
great teachers.

A great deal of engagement is shown to take place when technology and personalization are infused in the learning environment. That is the environment we want in every classroom every day. In Mike's district, the motto is Engage, Inspire, and Empower. They deliberately and intentionally measure/ inspect what they respect and aim to improve. For the past two years, they have been administering a student engagement survey to all students in grades three to eight (roughly 1,800 students each year).

The student engagement survey is administered in partnership with a research and training company. The survey itself is measuring themes aligned with Maslow's hierarchy of needs, and the results show degrees to which students feel safe, feel belonging, feel relevant, and so forth. These results are disaggregated and shared at the school level. Each principal is tasked with action planning and held accountable for results.

Annually each principal conducts review sessions and action planning with faculty and staff to address and respond to student voice. After the first year, students at all six campuses in the district shared that they wanted greater choice in demonstrating how they learn and they wanted school to be more relevant to their future needs. Data like this (from student voice) drives change in a learner-centered environment. In figure 7.1, we show the 2016 dimension results from choice and relevance. The dimension results combine and average responses for all questions in that particular dimension.

One of the questions on the survey from the Choice Dimension is "In class I get to choose the activities I work on." From 2015 to 2016, with action planning and deliberate awareness and improvement, the overall average response went from 2.76 to 3.07, an increase of 0.31. This is considered to be significant growth. With leadership and focus, everything can be accomplished. Engagement can be measured; student voice can be utilized and maximized.

One of the highlights of the execution of the student engagement survey is the fact that fifth-grade students had the opportunity to meet with the head of research and design in focus groups to react to and suggest readability improvements to the survey questions. Not only do we measure student engagement to elevate student voice and use it as a driver for change, but we use their voice to make sure the measurement is relevant and comprehensible as well.

Choice	The Choice dimension concerns the level of freedom that a student feels when he or she is deciding the types of assignments and projects that he or she will work on in class.	**3.09**
Relevance	Relevance statements measure how strongly a student feels that what he or she is learning in class is applicable and useful to his or her lives.	**3.17**

Figure 7.1 Choice and Relevance Dimension Results from Student Engagement Survey

WHY MEET INDIVIDUAL LEARNER NEEDS?

As superintendents, we strive to create environments that put structures in place that enable students to reap the benefits of being in the right place at the right time. The only way to do that is to ensure that every classroom is the right place all the time. Educators have a single school year to make a difference for students. Students only have one chance to experience each grade. This means we have around 180 days per year to facilitate impactful learning. We don't get do-overs. We have tremendous power over our students' lives, and we have a critical responsibility to ensure that they are in the right place at the right time.

Meeting individual students' needs is an often-elusive goal for American educators. For as long as we can remember, we've been learning about and promoting differentiated instruction or providing different students with varied approaches to learning. This lofty goal has remained quite challenging for many educators. One inherent structural challenge lies in the fact that the system itself is not and was not designed for individuals. Our industrial-era school system was designed for groups, not individuals.

Consider the classroom design of the typical schoolroom: rows of desks all pointed toward the front of the room. Group instruction is based on rigid and fixed schedules regulated by bells, mass movement of large groups of students, standardization of assessments, and batch organization of students. This is a model whereby the teacher generally teaches to the middle level so that the material is usually too hard for some, too easy for others, and possibly irrelevant for those who might be at the "right" level. That model served society well from the 1800s through the 1900s. This may have been true for most people but not for all learners.

Times are changing. Actually, times have changed. Scores of research reports inform the world about more effective ways to facilitate learning. The buzz around actual differentiation is growing. Educators and school systems are more interested in how to incorporate differentiation into their approach. The good news is that information on how to differentiate is all around us. Studies focusing on everything from neuroscience to instructional practices inform us of the need to change and the ability to do so.

Early in his career, Mike published an article that touched on the subject:

> With U.S. History Workshop, I was able to teach traditional units of instruction more effectively than before. For example, most U.S. history teachers are familiar with the Civil War and Reconstruction period (roughly 1850–1880). For this and every unit taught with the workshop, I taught the students to view social studies and history as human experiences. This unit, like the others, separates history into five core areas or themes: Civil Rights, Women in History,

Science & Technology, Politics, and War & Conflict. I identified key ideas, concepts and so on for each area and allowed student teams to explore these key concepts rather than the whole concept of the Civil War and Reconstruction. Instead of teaching this unit as one big complication, I presented it as one big puzzle—each of the concepts or ideas from each of the areas was like a piece of a puzzle. The challenge for the students was to piece together the puzzle independently, cooperatively, and with direction from the teacher. (p. 11)

That content and experience provide a conceptual background for our long-standing passion for meeting students where they are. Fast forward to 2017, and in classrooms around the world, we have differentiation, individualization, and personalization in the mix of instructional improvements. The movements now are hopefully going to transform an adult-centered system to a learner-centered system. A learner-centered system addresses learning needs of adults and children and is built on the foundational belief that all can learn and learn at their own pace.

Another example of differentiated instruction in modern contemporary practice comes from a third-grade classroom we visited recently. After viewing the video "Caine's Arcade," one teacher's classroom was inspired to spend thirty minutes a day for two weeks working on their voice projects. These students experienced a combination of differentiated instruction (different project for each child/group), individualized instruction (each child's unique voice and interest came alive in his or her projects), and personalized instruction (each child had full creative license to produce learning in his or her own ways).

In addition to this type of engaging and creative lesson planning, our school districts support a broad range of digital tools designed for meeting individual student needs. We have invested time, dollars, resources, planning, training, and support for this transformation of teaching. The example from third grade also shows what it looks like when student voices are part of the pedagogical equation.

To support differentiated instruction, our districts have intentionally and deliberately acquired digital resources. We use subscriptions, tools, and programs to support teachers and students. We use combinations of free, open, educational resources as well as paid resources. Some of the companies with whom we partner are web-based subscriptions, which allow for 24/7 school and home access. The possibilities are endless as we truly become a community of learners.

As a superintendent, I see learning every day and my aim is to support every classroom's transformation into an engaging, motivating, challenging learning space for our nation's most precious assets—our children. It's imperative that we act with urgency to provide the most excellent educational system for all children. (Retrieved from a blog post Mike wrote for Discovery Education: http://blog.discoveryeducation.com/blog/2015/12/02/defining-differentiation-in-todays-classroom/)

WHOSE LEARNING IS IT ANYWAY?

One of the "hot topics" of today in education is personalized learning. Does it mean that we let students learn whatever they want, whenever they want? Does it mean we change educational structures midstream without discussing the changes with the students? In this chapter, we'll explore concepts to allow student voice to help direct the complex decisions and change associated with personalized learning. Our concept of personalized learning is one in which there is a combination of individual learner needs, teacher expertise, and student choice in demonstrating how students know, understand, and apply concepts.

As we dive into the larger concept of personalized learning, we look to contemporary research, literature, examples, and best practices. Our dive includes visits across the country and world in search of learning systems that support and meet the needs of all learners. We again look to Education Reimagined and their "North Star" for a look at their main compass points: Personalized, Relevant, Contextual. This learning is an approach that uses such factors as the learner's own passions, strengths, needs, family, culture, and community as fuel for the development of knowledge, skills, and dispositions.

> One big problem: proponents have struggled to define personalized learning, let alone demonstrate its effectiveness. The purpose, tools, and instructional techniques that make up the notion vary considerably, depending who you ask. While a fair amount of research exists on specific personalization strategies, such as the use of adaptive math software, the literature includes very little on personalized learning as a comprehensive approach. (Retrieved from https://fs24.formsite.com/edweek/images/Spotlight-Personalized-Learning-2017-Sponsored.pdf)

Learning experiences are leveraged to bridge gaps and meet learning challenges; designed to expand interests, opportunities, and perspectives; and be responsive to learners' passions. At the same time, they are rooted in real-world contexts and empower the learner to demonstrate his or her learning in a variety of authentic ways and settings. From Education Reimagined (2015), "A Transformational Vision for Education in the US," the authors state:

> Personalized, relevant, and contextualized learning also acknowledges that different learners face different challenges to learning, whether in health, safety,

economic situation, emotional wellbeing, social interactions, or competency development. Those challenges are both identified and addressed so that the learner is adequately supported, thus ensuring that his or her current life situation does not constrain the breadth or depth of learning.

Personalized, relevant, and contextualized learning is one of the cornerstones of the reimagined vision for education. See figure 0.1 in the preface for a review of the "North Star" components.

So what is personalized learning? In their book, *Personalizing 21st Century Education: A Framework for Student Success*, Brown, Domenech, and Sherman (2016) state:

> There is no agreement on one definition. In most cases, today personalized learning refers to some form of blended learning in which software programs are used that adapt to the ability level of a child. It may also be used to define programs in which the teacher employs differentiated instruction. These are approximations of what personalized learning could be at the classroom level, but they do not encompass the systemic transformation that we envision. (p. 6)

In our version of personalized learning, we envision a transformation in how children are taught and how the system organizes for learning. Each child is treated as a unique individual, and his or her education begins with the development of a personalized education plan. The child is assessed in each of the subjects to be taught and, based on the assessments, integrated lesson plans are developed that build on what the child already knows, with instructional strategies designed for his or her ability level.

Other examples of personalized learning come from projects. Elementary school teacher Donna Kinley's WESN news project was another initiative that was totally student driven. Donna had the students research and decide on the positions necessary to produce a newscast. She had them write resumes and fill out applications for the positions they chose to apply for that best fit their personalities and talents.

In speaking with the library information specialist Andrea Lathan, she reported, "The students chose the stories they felt were important to cover Wilmot School's student activities. The students did the interviewing, filming and editing to create the newscast. Here is a link to the last *newscast* http://bit.do/WESNVideo; look what these amazing kids produced on their own!"

WHAT DO STUDENTS THINK?

In Mike's district at one of the middle schools, there was a new structural concept started in August 2017. Joining the existing two grade-level teams will be a hybrid called Team Fusion. This is being designed as a unique, personalized, and innovative learning experience for a cohort of up to 30 eighth-grade students at Caruso Middle School.

Aligned with the district's new mission to "provide innovative educational experiences of the highest quality that engage, inspire and empower each student to excel and contribute to improving the world," Team Fusion will allow students to coauthor part of their eighth-grade learning experience and be immersed in an environment with limitless growth opportunities.

Initially, the plan was for students on Team Fusion to experience an authentic, integrated approach to academic learning in the areas of ELA, social studies, and science under the guidance of the Team Fusion lead teacher, and would have left for their math class. During Encore (exploratory/elective) class periods, students from Team Fusion will integrate with eighth-grade students from all teams.

Team Fusion students will experience more flexibility in their day as they collaborate with their lead teacher to determine where to focus their time and learning. In addition to this integrated, flexible model, Team Fusion students will benefit from a personalized learning experience where the students collaborate with their lead teacher to identify goals and monitor progress.

Because students on Team Fusion will have one lead teacher for multiple core subjects, the curriculum will be integrated to combine multiple content areas into the learning experience. This design will allow for project-based learning experiences where students work over time to understand and respond to engaging and complex questions, problems, or challenges.

After holding parent education sessions, student groups, and individual conferences and after reviewing survey data, the plan for fusion changed from a three-hour block with three replacement classes (ELA, science, and social studies) to a two-hour block with two replacement classes (social studies and ELA). Student voice changed the plan!

Overview of Team Fusion

Goal:

- Provide a unique personalized, innovative, and engaging learning experience for a cohort of eighth-grade students.

Structure:

- Originally, all students will have ELA, science, and social studies with the same *core* teacher—after reviewing input, including student input, the plan changed as mentioned.

- Students will receive math instruction on the blue or white team with a different teacher.
- Students will receive *Encore* instruction with *Encore* teachers.

Instruction Will Include:

- Personalized learning where the student becomes a self-directed learner who identifies goals, contributes to the design of their learning, monitors progress, and analyzes attainment of their goals
- Project-based learning experiences where students work over time to understand and respond to an engaging and complex question, problem, or challenge
- Problem-based learning experiences where students collaborate together to solve open-ended problems
- Integrated curriculum that combines multiple content areas into the learning experience (i.e., studying the atomic bomb from a scientific and historical context or utilization of the *Big History Project* online curriculum integrates social studies and science learning with PBL activities in each unit)
- Flexible schedules that allow students and the teacher to best determine where to focus their time and learning within the *core* block
- Focus on the 4Cs—collaboration, critical thinking, creativity, and communication
- Student engagement as a priority and emphasis throughout the course of the year
- Inclusion of the standards—Common Core State Standards for English/Language Arts, Next Generation Science Standards, Illinois Standards for Social Studies

Student Selection:

- Families will complete an application to be considered for this offering.
- Up to thirty students will be selected.
- Class composition will, as closely as possible, represent the demographic composition of the school's student body.

Intended Outcomes:

- Increased student ownership in their own learning and growth (pre-posttest)
- Increased student engagement (as measured by data analytics with research partner)
- Make expected academic growth (as measured by academic assessments)

Figure 7.2 contains student responses to application questions for the opt-in class Team Fusion. This input as well as focus group and interview input compelled the leadership team to modify the originally planned three-hour block into the two-hour block.

Students and parents expressed concern about having to be in the same classroom with the same teacher for three hours per day, so they changed this to a two-hour time block. Students and parents expressed concern about not

Why do you believe this program would benefit you?	What idea or ideas do you have to make Team Fusion the best experience possible?
Ability to solve more complex problems in collaboration with other students or teachers	Discussing current economic and legal topics in group setting, learning more different types of sound waves
I think that I would benefit from a program like this because it would team to solve problems in the real world. When I did pentathlon in California . . . we did integrative learning across subject lines and I loved this . . . it was how I learned best . . . I thought I would not be able to do this, but I actually learned better. It made sense to me.	We could do team-bonding activities that include problem-based learning . . . across subjects and collaborate as a group while still doing independent learning. Because we also have different learning styles and abilities, seeing how others problem solve would be a good experience for me. I also maybe could help other kids find unique ways to learn.
It seems like fun and interesting.	Don't know.
I like to learn at my own pace. I like bonding with my teachers. I like learning everything together at the same pace.	I'm excited to do group projects and I think I can be a great teammate. I know a lot of team building games, and I would be happy to lead them to make our team stronger.
Having to do the projects and join the different subject would help me have a better understanding of each of them. It would also help me connect the subjects to the world.	Make the learning environment beneficial and have the classroom interactive to give us the best angle at the topic.
I believe that this program would help me see how different academic subjects are intertwined. I believe this program would help strengthen my academic and social skills.	I think this program would help get me more involved in my education, so I would work harder. I think it would be great to be involved in this new program and make it a success. I would work hard both for myself and my Fusion classmates to make this program fun and successful.

Figure 7.2 Student Responses to Application Questions for Team Fusion

Why do you believe this program would benefit you?	What idea or ideas do you have to make Team Fusion the best experience possible?
Name Omitted says, "Test taking causes me a lot of stress. I don't feel prepared most of the time. When I know a teacher well and they know me, I feel less anxious. It's been great showing my learning through projects."	Have students pick which standards and help make the rubrics for grading.
It would challenge me in different ways I haven't been challenged before. It would make me think outside the box and it would be something that made me work and think harder. I think this program would benefit me in different ways and I would thrive from this experience.	I would like the teacher having an open mind. If we have an idea on a project or paper, the teacher wouldn't mind us doing it, and maybe even helping us bring the idea to the next level, so it challenges us in different ways.
I think it would benefit me because this program will let me work at my own pace and have me learn at my own level.	It will be great being involved in a new program. Being flexible and having an open mind will make this a great experience.
There is more one-on-one teacher time. I also like to be creative and it sounds like this will give the chance to do that.	I'm really interested in video game design and want to major in video game design in college. I would like to learn skills that are related to that goal.
My favorite classes at Caruso have been my science classes in sixth and seventh grades. I like how the teacher teaches us the main ideas and then gives us time to work on our projects until they are complete and we think our projects have met the standards. I like having the time to complete it on my own timeline and making sure it is the best I can do.	A positive teacher works to get to know me. I want a teacher to teach me, not just get me started and leave me alone to get the work done by myself.
I believe this program would benefit me by having one teacher and choosing to study a variety of things that you are passionate about.	Doing whatever it takes to get the students engaged. Recognizing the different capabilities and passions of the students.
I believe more 1:1 time with the teacher will help me, and I also believe the integrated learning and the three hours of one big core class will help me with time management skills. Also I believe that the projects that have to do with integrated learning will help me because instead of focusing on three small projects, it will be easier for me to focus on one big project instead of dividing my attention.	An idea that I have is to use the integrated learning to do interactive projects and make learning more fun. Also to have the curriculum standards based but to have the students decide whether they want all three classes or just two classes put into one for projects and lots of group work on large assignments and projects.

Figure 7.2 (Continued)

Why do you believe this program would benefit you?	*What idea or ideas do you have to make Team Fusion the best experience possible?*
I want to try something new and different.	A teacher who is educated in most subjects.
I am hoping that Team Fusion will be a good fit for me; I am uncertain of all the benefits. I am currently bored, distracted, and a bit too social in the current classroom style. I want to succeed in school and hope this will be a better way for me to learn.	I enjoy putting PowerPoint slides together and giving class presentations. I would like to use these skills as a resource for a team project.
I believe it would benefit me because I would be learning language arts and social studies at the same time. This makes it easier because the two classes are already so similar. Having both at once would make learning and doing projects easier because it wouldn't be two similar things, it would be one that's both.	I think that Team Fusion already sounds like it's going to be a good experience.

Figure 7.2 (Continued)

knowing the curriculum, so they are going to establish up to two, two-hour blocks that will replace a student's ELA and social studies classes with the integrated *Big History Project* curriculum.

Finally, students and parents expressed concern about the relevancy and preparation of this to the high school because this World Studies course is a prelude to an American Studies course (ELA/social sciences) at the high school.

Team Fusion has more resources at https://www.smore.com/7hypq-cms-team-fusion.

ASK'EM

Ask: Ask students in multiple formats for their views. Then act on their views and share with them what and how was impacted by their voice.

Support: Support innovative and inventive principals and teachers and students as you dream up, create, form, and do personalized learning pilots and initiatives.

Know: What challenges are you addressing or attempting to address with inventive programming? If you are trying to improve student perceptions of relevance, be sure to create a working definition of relevance and work in concert to make changes.

Empower: Empower students to help write or revise survey questions. Ask students to join with teacher teams to review practices and recommend changes. Enlist student support at Board of Education presentations.

Monitor: If it is important to your organization, then measure it. If you don't have a measure, find one or create one. If you monitor, you will be able to replicate that which works well and amend that which can be changed and terminate that which is not working.

SUMMARY

The learning purposes of this book include establish, propose, and reinforce the "how" and the "why" for including student voice in leadership decision making and provide leaders with actionable case studies and examples from the field for implementation. In the first part of the book, the focus was on the technological impact of modern education and the move to personalized learning.

So far in the seven chapters, we have addressed Student Voice in Governance, Service, and Character Education, Student Voice in Technology Instruction, and in this section of the book, we addressed Student Voice in Design and Communication.

With the focus in chapter 7 on the personalized learning movement as well as input from student voice from a recent pilot application, we continue to show how to make student voice move from invisible to invaluable. In this chapter, we identified why engaged learning matters for students. We identified measures and metrics for getting baseline data for action planning and continuous improvement.

Although personalized learning is itself a concept in development, we share a real-life example of a plan for integrating a new model that includes personalized learning as a starting point toward transformation. Another example of personalized learning and hearing from students is found in the following "podcast" recording describing eighth-grade students engaging in trigonometry using light poles in the school's field: http://bit.do/trigonometryingrade8.

Excerpts of student voice:

> We are trying to find distance/elevation—this is trigonometry—using measures of angles and heights to see how this corresponds with the world—Q—how did you guys decide to do this? Student: kind of mentioned if you look up at the sky it looks like the sky is falling . . . it's far more interactive, we get to do something beyond looking at a computer screen—now we have a chance to apply ourselves . . . the pole caught our attention.

The student experience as captured in the audio file is related to one of the "North Star" tenets from the Education Reimagined Transformative Vision.

This is a guiding and foundational document to which we have referred throughout our book, one of the "North Star" tenets (see Figure 0.1 in the Preface) is Personalized, Relevant and Contextualized:

From https://education-reimagined.org, p. 7:

PERSONALIZED, RELEVANT, AND CONTEXTUALIZED learning is an approach that uses such factors as the learner's own passions, strengths, needs, family, culture, and community as fuel for the development of knowledge, skills, and dispositions. Learning experiences are leveraged to bridge gaps and meet learning challenges; designed to expand interests, opportunities, and perspectives; and responsive to learners' passions. At the same time, they are rooted in real-world contexts and empower the learner to demonstrate his or her learning in a variety of authentic ways and settings.

As we engage student voice in leadership and as we transform learning from adult/teacher-centered to learner/student-centered, it's imperative that we not only understand the vision, but we can operationalize and execute the vision too! Another set of suggestions from students is shared in the following audio file: https://youtu.be/SRfAhylZTN4 (excerpts shared below):

let the classroom be more open ended . . . here you are just—you have to come up with your project, you have to learn from yourself—we have to learn how to learn for ourselves—teacher is there for support . . . we did not even start using the machines, we learned about them we first had to learn about nanoscience (content)—once we were given the tools we needed we were set loose . . . let the student follow his passion—allowed to fail—allowed to learn from real world connections . . . Q - At what age do you think we should create learner centered environments . . . A—any age is OK—we have voice to change our schedules . . . listen to the students—listen to the students—they have opinions and valid—a lot of times they (students) get left out of decisions—though we (students) are affected by the decisions . . . I learned to love science!

The audio files show real-life examples of "ASK'EM."

GUEST COMMENTARY FROM DR. ANTHONY MCCONNELL, ASSISTANT SUPERINTENDENT FOR TEACHING, LEARNING, & INNOVATION—DEERFIELD PUBLIC SCHOOLS DISTRICT 109

Anthony shares an impressive narrative about student agency in his school. The impromptu narrative is full of wonder and agency. This commentary shows an example of real-life personalized learning experiences that elementary students engaged in organically and meaningfully. When we create environments conducive to engaged, personalized learning, magic happens!

Let Go . . . Sit Back . . . Watch . . . And Let Kids Be Amazing (Published by Anthony McConnell on March 27, 2017)

Several months ago I requested a special item as part of a grant through the Deerfield Education Foundation. The item was a K'NEX Ferris Wheel. But this wasn't just any normal Ferris Wheel. Oh no. This Ferris wheel had over 8,500 pieces, and when finished would stand 6 feet tall. Oh, and did I also mention that it is motorized so it will actually rotate when switched on. I had first seen this creation at a school in Colorado about two years ago and I was so impressed that students had built it.

The Foundation was gracious enough to approve our grant along with the Ferris Wheel. It came in around November if I remember correctly but I wasn't exactly sure how to organize students to build it. I thought and thought about how to do it. I asked around to teachers and Mrs. Schippers, the Library Information Specialist, to see which students really liked K'NEX. I thought about asking specific students but I wanted to give all kids a chance to be involved that wanted to and not just a few. I thought about how to go about the process of building this monstrosity and getting as many students involved as I could most of December and winter break. I was reminded of it every time I went to the library and saw the enormous box that contained the more than 8,500 pieces. I was also a little concerned as the age suggestion for this project was 16+. Days became weeks and all that was to show was a box of 8,500 individual pieces taking up space behind the library desk.

One day while talking to Mrs. Schippers and Mrs. Pfeffer, Library Assistant, I was reminded of one of my favorite TED Talks from Sugata Mitra, professor of educational technology at Newcastle University. Mr. Mitra is the mind behind the "hole in the wall computers" in rural villages in India. An amazing thing happened when he simply installed these computers in the walls of buildings and walked away. Students began to play with them and learn on their own with no adult guidance. So, I thought why not take the same approach with the Ferris Wheel. Kipling's own little "hole in the wall' project.

One day in January I gathered up almost two dozen bins, opened up the large box of pieces and placed them by color in the bins. Our makerspace was full of bins with over 8,500 K'NEX pieces just sitting on the table and the floor. I looked at the all of the pieces and then dropped the 40 page instruction manual in the middle of the table and walked away—determined to just watch and see what happened.

As I walked away I even had a moment right out of Sugata Mitra's experience with the hole in wall computers. A student had wandered over from the Smartlab and asked me what all the stuff was. Acting clueless I said "I don't really know, they sent it to us in the mail. Looks complicated though." And then I left.

Over the next two months I waited and watched. What transpired amazed me. I watched students pick up the instructions and work on the project on their own. Sometimes it was just one student, sometimes a group of 10–12. In all I saw probably over 40–50 different 3rd, 4th, and 5th graders working on it in some way. And that was just the kids that I saw. Some students took the lead and organized others to work as a team. Other times a single student would work on a piece when they had a free minute. Regardless, when the next person or group came they evaluated the progress and picked right up where the other person(s) had left off. They worked on it during library time, after their SmartLab projects were finished, and at indoor recess. Whenever, there was a free minute someone picked up the task of building the project.

I was out of town one Friday when I received the message that the students had completed it. In a little over 2 months, students working together solved the problems, overcame the setbacks, and created the 6-foot-tall project with nearly no adult guidance.

I said I am amazed but I shouldn't be surprised. This is once again evidence of students rising to the occasion when given the opportunity. But it did get me thinking about some lessons from this experience that I think are applicable to all educators and even parents. Here are my 4 major takeaways.

1. Put challenging opportunities in front of students. Do not be dissuaded by the scope of a project or by student's age. They are capable of so much more than we give them credit for. If something is going to hold them back let it not be the adults.
2. Let go. Resist the desire to control the project and the learning. Be comfortable if something seems a little messy and disorganized. There will be setbacks. Do not let that be a reason for an adult to jump in and "solve it" for the students. Big projects take time. Be patient.
3. Do not force collaboration. If a challenge is sufficient collaboration will happen naturally because it has to. Create challenges where the project and solutions are bigger than any one individual. Let students naturally discover the need for good communication and collaboration through necessity not direction.
4. Encouragement is maybe the most important gift we can give our children. They do not need us to solve all the problems nor do they need us to simply tell them they can do it. They need us to actually believe they can do it and then speak and act accordingly.

Remember, that our kids are capable of much more than we give them credit for. Just give them the chance. Sometimes it is okay to throw the pieces on the table and just walk away.

Part IV

STUDENT VOICE IN EQUITY
AND EVALUATION

Chapter 8

Helping Students Define Equity: Engage Students in the Equity Discussion

When we create schools that work for kids, the tone of discourse about learning changes so opportunities to innovate, create, and pursue passions become the norm rather than the exception.

—Sanfelippo and Sinanis (2016)

Student Voice—Literally
Student Involvement
Graduation
The Evolution of Equity in Schools
Summary
Guest Commentary from Recent Graduate Charlie Zielinski

Reflection Questions

When is it okay to have certain programs or opportunities in your schools that only certain students are able to participate?

How do you balance the input of adults and students when addressing issues of equity in schools?

Why is it important for our world that we encourage, support, and amplify student voice in regard to equitable treatment of all people?

Stop-Think-Act

Stop: How does your district currently evaluate issues of student equity?

Think: Why might it be important to engage student voice as you think about how you ensure equitable treatment of students?

Act: Identify a way to increase student advocacy and involvement when it comes to equity in your school or school district.

EQUALITY | EQUITY

Figure 8.1 Fair/Equal

Every student in our country is entitled to a free and appropriate public education. That word *appropriate* begins to get at the concept of equity. When you allow student voice into the equity discussion, students can learn to self-advocate for what is appropriate for them.

Most educators have seen the image shown in figure 8.1, or at least some image similar to it. The concept is that equal treatment of all students doesn't always appropriately meet their unique needs. Equitable treatment identifies each student's unique needs and helps to bridge gaps and provide all students with their best possible education.

We see this process play out in course selection, individual education plans (IEPs), interventions, assistive technology, one-on-one aides, systems of support, gifted programming, and myriad other ways in our schools. Traditionally, however, it is the adults in the system who identify the need for the wooden boxes in the image. In this chapter, we will explore the power of engaging student voice in the equity conversation.

STUDENT VOICE—LITERALLY

In just about every high school across the country, you will find a theater program. You can count on staples such as tryouts, rehearsals, opening nights, musical numbers, and standing ovations. Students bring their voice to the stage and they perform. Like many other school programs, theater provides a community, a sense of belonging, and family atmosphere for the students who participate.

What happens when a student has a voice, but that voice comes out in a different language? Is the theater program simply not for them? That question was asked at Leyden High School District several years ago in suburban Chicago where 65 percent of the students are Latino. Within that group, many of the students are first-generation students in the United States and English language learners.

According to the National Center for Education Statistics, "Extracurricular activities provide a channel for reinforcing the lessons learned in the classroom, offering students the opportunity to apply academic skills in a real-world context, and are thus considered part of a well-rounded education. Recent research suggests that participation in extracurricular activities may increase students' sense of engagement or attachment to their school, and thereby decrease the likelihood of school failure and dropping out" (retrieved from https://nces.ed.gov/pubs95/web/95741.asp).

If those benefits exist for students who get involved, is it equitable that 65 percent of Leyden's students cannot participate in a theater program simply because their "voice" comes out in a different language?

From that idea, Teatro Leyden was born. When tryouts occur, two casts are selected. One cast will eventually perform in English, while the other cast will perform the show in Spanish. When time comes to perform the show on a Saturday, the 4:00 p.m. show might feature the English-speaking cast and the 7:00 p.m. show might feature the Spanish-speaking cast. Not only does this approach allow double the number of students to get involved, but it also provides a literal voice to a whole different group of students and allows them to find a place in their school community. It gives more equitable access to all of the benefits listed earlier.

Now that Teatro Leyden has been in place for a number of years, the success stories are many. One such story involves a student named Maria.

STUDENT INVOLVEMENT

Maria was born in Guatemala where she lived with her family until she was twelve years old. Following some extraordinary tragedies in her family, Maria came to live with her sister in the United States. She knew no one, she didn't speak English, and she found herself in a new place with new schools and new faces.

During her junior year, Teatro Leyden would be performing *La Gringa*, an award-winning production about a young woman (named Maria) who moved to the United States from Puerto Rico only to find that she didn't feel like she truly belonged in the United States or in her native Puerto Rico.

Maria's Spanish teacher gave her the script for *La Gringa* and told her to read it as homework as she wanted her to try out for the play. Maria was apprehensive, but she learned the lines and showed up at for tryouts. She didn't just make the cast; she was given the lead in the play. Maria from Guatemala was going to take the stage and "play" Maria from Puerto Rico. The show was a great success, and Maria also went on to play the lead role in Sandra Cisneros's *The House on Mango Street* during her senior year.

As Maria developed her voice on stage, she also decided to use her voice to start to make some changes in her school. After experiencing what it felt like to get involved in extracurricular programs, she looked around and noticed that many of her non-English-speaking classmates were not finding ways to get connected in similar ways. She approached the administration and asked permission to start the ExcELLence Club. Her idea was to bring together English Language Learning students (hence the capital ELL) for regular meetings. She wanted to help them find sports and clubs that they could join in order to get involved in the schools.

She found that, with a little bit of support, her classmates would find a place where they could fit in and contribute. She used her voice to help promote equity. Even though Maria has graduated (and gone on to a full ride college scholarship), the club remains in place and more and more students are blazing trails and helping each other when it comes to student involvement.

GRADUATION

The annual graduation ceremony is an event that almost always features student voice. In some schools, the valedictorian or salutatorian steps up to the podium and delivers a prepared speech. In other schools, the students might vote to select a class representative to make a speech. In most cases, the attendees are able to hear the thoughts of either highly successful or highly popular members of the graduating class.

Another speech that is typically featured at a graduation ceremony comes from the superintendent. During that time frame, you might expect some motivational words, some famous quotes, and some talk about the future. When Nick arrived at Leyden, he found a very different tradition for the superintendent's remarks. For more than twenty years, the theme of that speech has been centered on the idea that there are many paths to success.

The way it works is that the building administration in each high school selects three students who represent unique pathways throughout their four years in high school. Some might have been extremely high achievers academically or athletically. Others may have overcome a seemingly insurmountable obstacle. Their stories are as unique as the students themselves. The superintendent interviews each of those students in order to tell their stories at the graduation ceremony.

Many times, the featured students' classmates have no idea about some aspects of their stories. For the younger brothers and sisters in the crowd, and for the parents, grandparents, and loved ones, the stories serve to provide motivation and hope for all students. It's not uncommon to see teachers, students, and parents crying during the ceremony.

If equity is a goal in schools, this tradition takes student voice, pairs it with the superintendent's voice, and shares a message that there isn't one right way to "do" high school. Schools are for everyone, and no matter what barriers might present themselves, success can be achieved and has been achieved. Because those students are willing to share their voice and their stories, you cannot measure the impact it has on inspiring others to follow their lead.

THE EVOLUTION OF EQUITY IN SCHOOLS

Equity is a moving target in schools. It's not something you figure out and then announce equity has been achieved. If we look throughout history, we'll find times that different groups have had to fight for equitable treatment with others. Significant legislation such as *Brown v. Board of Education* in 1954, the Civil Rights Act of 1964, the Voting Rights Act of 1965, and countless others mark national efforts to provide equity.

In our local schools, we should constantly be evaluating our practices. Should more female students have opportunities to learn coding and high-level math and science? Should more male students have a chance to take childcare or culinary arts classes?

Gender equity seems obvious, but issues can become more controversial when you address racial or religious equity, equity related to sexual preference, equitable opportunities for students with special needs, and more. (The end of this chapter features a student commentary about the importance of student voice and navigating the complex topic of transgender students.)

No school will have the same demographics or needs from one year to the next. We cannot expect that our current practices will meet the needs of our future students. If we can agree that change is constant, then we also have to agree that our role in ensuring equity is constantly changing too. The adults in an organization cannot and should not try to figure all of this out on their own. Our students have experiences and perspectives that we do not have.

Their voices must be part of the process, because after all, they are why we do what we do.

ASK'EM

Ask: Ask your students to share the experiences they have had in your schools and about the experiences they have seen others have.

Support: Student voice comes in the form of new ideas and potential changes. We are willing to take risks and support their ideas, especially when they are trying to help the district achieve higher levels of equity.

Know: We need to know what is happening in districts around us, across the country, and across the world. If we take the time to learn about what others are doing, we can adapt successful practices and allow them to benefit our students as well.

Empower: As leaders, we need to construct the opportunities for student voice to intersect with equity issues. We cannot twiddle our thumbs and wait for it to happen. We need to empower our students by putting them in situations to participate in the process.

Monitor: Equity is a moving target and so are the needs of our students. We need to monitor constantly how we are doing, what changes are necessary, and how we can include student voice in that conversation.

SUMMARY

Equity means many things. It might refer to the opportunities you provide to students. It might refer to the supports you put in place to help students be successful. It might refer to how you allocate limited resources to best meet the needs of all students. Equity is multifaceted, complex, and ever-changing.

Equity in schools isn't something you ever get to check off a list as being done. New issues and new needs will present themselves every year that you work in education. The important thing to remember is, if our students are to be the recipients of ethical treatment, they should have voice in how we get there.

GUEST COMMENTARY FROM RECENT GRADUATE CHARLIE ZIELINSKI

Starting high school is a different experience for everyone. Some people get more immature, or some people get more mature, but everyone gets a voice from their experience in high school. The students get a voice from their peers, or sometimes their faculty. My high school experience was all around a positive experience.

I knew kids that had a bad experience in high school, but most of it was because of the people that they surrounded themselves with. The staff always wanted to do what was best for the kids. They knew that that is how to truly help a student grow.

East Leyden high school's motto is "What's Best for the Kids," and they really strive to keep that true by building a good community of acceptance around the entire school. When I first started high school, I knew the school promoted equality, but they did it at a light scale. Compared to my middle school, promoting any sense of equality, even if it was on a light scale, was good enough to make me comfortable in school.

When I was in middle school, I learned that I wasn't like everyone else. I started learning about myself and trying to make myself more comfortable. I struggled with depression and my self-image ever since I was in elementary school, so trying to make myself more comfortable was hard. I started exploring my sexuality and my gender and that's when I learned about the term "transgender."

I knew I was different than everyone else, which made me even more uncomfortable. After learning more about that term, I realized I was transgender and I knew the only way to make myself feel better was to come out and start going by a different name and different pronouns.

I talked to my school administration letting them know that I wanted to come out as transgender. The middle school wasn't much help, stating that it was just a phase to me and my mom. They were an authority figure saying that what I felt was wrong. I listened to them. My voice was taken away. I was crushed. I went back into my closed off self.

Coming into high school, I could sense a different environment as soon as I walked through the door on my first day. I could sense the environment was calmer. I could sense more freedom. I didn't know exactly what made the environment like this, maybe it was because I was surrounded by a lot of people that I didn't know, or maybe it was because the staff pushed for an environment that protected every student and gave everyone a voice.

I always thought it was the students that helped make an environment like that, but as high school went by, I realized that it was the staff and the administration that made that environment. They were truly committed to make every student feel accepted. During my sophomore year of high school, I started getting more comfortable again.

I was ready to come out as transgender again. I knew that the high school's environment was different than my middle school, but I still didn't think I would get accepted right away. It took a lot of time and courage for me to become comfortable with coming out again.

After I talked to a school counselor, I was accepted right away. The counselor talked with me about how I felt and we came up with a clear plan for my future here at Leyden to make me feel safe and comfortable. She talked to all of my teachers and she let them know I wanted to go by Charlie and I wanted them to use different pronouns. She talked to my dean and let him know to make sure I am safe and not bullied, and then she talked with my principal and assistant principal and tried to make an arrangement to get me to use a bathroom I am more comfortable using.

The school actually gave me a voice that I kept hidden away for so long. They accepted me and went above and beyond by giving me people I can talk to about this. After I talked to my counselor, I saw immediate change the following day. My teachers were all calling me by my preferred name, Charlie, and they asked me if there is anything they could personally do to make school more of a safe place for me. I knew that I could talk to any of my teachers if I ever had a problem, and I knew that I wasn't going to have any problems because the environment that they promoted got stronger after they learned about just how diverse every student is.

After coming out, I noticed signs on almost every teacher's door, or in their classroom, marking that the classroom, and the teacher, is a safe space for LGBT students. I had students, some who I have never talked to, finally interested in my life and what I had to say.

I finally had a voice because my feelings and who I am was finally validated by someone who had authority. I finally found someone to help me understand who I am and help me become more mature. It was the staff of East Leyden that made the biggest impact on my life. The staff had such a positive attitude with clear communication with all of the students. They promoted the environment that made me feel comfortable in the first place, and they enforced that environment every chance they had.

By having that environment of equity and equality all around, it encouraged more students to come out. I personally helped two students come out as transgender too. They had a harder time than I did, but after hearing my experience and how smoothly it went, they came out as well. Because the school accepted such a small minority of students, it gave us a voice that we didn't even know we had.

I didn't have a voice in middle school, I didn't have a voice when I first started high school. When I was accepted by someone other than my friends, and I thought that I could be myself, I got the voice that was kept from me.

It was important to have this environment in school because if this environment of acceptance and equality was never put in place, I wouldn't be the person that I am today. I would still feel shy and antisocial, but instead I opened up more and started expressing myself. It makes the student feel more validated, instead of voiceless.

Something so simple as having teachers call me by my preferred name gave me the validation I needed to become a more mature person with a voice that I realized could make a difference. At East Leyden, every single student has that voice. The school just has to do something to bring that voice out, and East Leyden knows how to do that with their community of acceptance, equity, and equality.

Chapter 9

Teacher Evaluation: Give Students a Voice

You know if education is good for one thing, it's good for making excuses.

—Eric Sheninger

Feedback
Excuse Elimination
Elevating Student Voice—Making It Invaluable
Takeaways and Lessons Learned
Next Steps
A Quick Note to Teachers Reading This Book
Summary

Reflection Questions

We are asked for feedback on our experience while golfing, receiving an oil change, or even having major surgery. These are areas where we may have no expertise, but still organizations want our feedback. Why do we not offer the same opportunity to our students?

What is the absolute worst thing that could happen if students had a voice on teacher performance?

If we were "inventing" school today, do you think we would create a system where students have no formal process to share their experiences with their teacher or do we simply accept a system because it is the one that has been traditionally handed down to us?

Schools preach innovation as a core competency or value yet are hesitant to implement something that makes common sense until someone else establishes a best practice or framework to follow. Do you have the courage to be different in your classroom or in your school?

Stop-Think-Act

Stop: Evaluation of teachers has simply become a process that schools "get through." It is time to take a moment to pause to critically analyze our intent, behaviors, and outcomes to see if they align.

Think: Students spend considerably more time with teachers than other entity or stakeholder group. However, schools have systematically excluded them from the process that is designed to measure how well they serve students!

Act: Work with your students to create a system that allows for student voice in teacher evaluations.

FEEDBACK

In the past several months, we have stayed at several different hotels seemingly all under a different parent brand or company. Universally, in the following days, we will likely receive an e-mail asking us to complete a survey about our experience. We are typically dutiful survey completers knowing the value they can add to the organization, and we still believe that karma will be impacted if we do not pay forward the fact that so many people completed surveys for us in our own research. Every once in a while, however, we hit delete on the customer survey e-mail as we may have what feels like 2,000 other e-mails to return.

When we do this, do you know what happens? They do not stop! Over and over again, we receive reminder e-mails until they guilt us into taking the four-minute survey. At this point, they typically have us convinced that they care. Perhaps they care about response rate, but perhaps they really care about what we have to say. We are typically positive people and generally record nice things to say.

A few weeks ago when checking in at a conference, however, PJ became frustrated that he had to wait several minutes as the desk attendant attempted to locate his "Loyalty" program identification number. He shared in the online survey that he would assume with the identifying information provided in the reservation, name, address, and so on that their system should automatically check if he is part of their Loyalty program before arrival in the case either he or his assistant neglected to tell them when making reservations. Is this lazy? Perhaps. Is this entitled? Probably. But hey—they asked.

What happened next was amazing. They replied with a personal e-mail and said they would do better. That was nice, in and of itself. Then, during the next several stays with this chain of hotels, PJ has been welcomed under the

Loyalty program whether he self-identified upon reservation or not. Not only did they listen, but they cared and they adjusted too.

We have had similar experiences following doctor visits, major surgery, oil changes, and even after visiting a restaurant. We are left with one major takeaway from all of these experiences: Individual feedback matters because they care about each of us as a customer regardless of individual expertise or knowledge in the particular field of service they are providing.

Let's juxtapose this to how we treat our students. We operate as if we do not trust them or worse, even care about their opinions. When is the last time we have requested students to give frank feedback about the service they are receiving or to voice concerns regarding their overall learning experience? In some schools and districts, the answer is never. In others, there may be a survey or two given throughout the year.

But very rarely will any process or instrument exist to provide feedback as to the service or effectiveness of a particular individual. Schools, school leaders, and teachers can make a plethora of excuses as to why this does not occur. At the root of every excuse is simply fear: fear of failure, fear of emotional distress, and fear of student retribution. One thing is for absolute certain, we cannot let fear dictate how we run schools or serve students, or we will never make the progress that is necessary to stay relevant in our ever-changing world.

EXCUSE ELIMINATION

A barrier to progress personally or in any organization is the use of excuses. When attempting to implement any idea that brings with it significant change, excuses often come to the forefront. We imagine even the most progressive of you reading this book thought of at least one excuse why using student feedback in teacher evaluation would not work simply upon reading the title of the chapter.

Think about that. If you are reading this book, you are clearly an advocate for student voice, yet doubt, fear, and excuses still creep forward. That is exactly why this section is included. Let's not ignore that voice. Let's bring forth all the reasons people may say this cannot work and rationally eviscerate those arguments.

- Students will seek revenge or retribution.

  - The data say that the 2010 MET project notes that student feedback about teachers is more consistent than those provided by administrators after classroom observation or those based solely on student test scores.

- What does that really mean? Of course, some students are going to skew their score to negatively evaluate a teacher they do not like. What the data from the MET project shows us is that such behavior is an outlier and is quite possibly no different from an administrator entering a room with a preconceived notion to the effectiveness of the teacher.

- Students do not want this responsibility.

  - The data say that in 2011, after a U.S. Department of Education listening tour, 94 percent of students noted the need for student input in teacher evaluation.
  - What does that really mean? We think it may be fair to say that most students do not want the stress of having to determine if someone is to be retained or terminated. We also think it is fair to say that they do not expect to have such authority. Giving a formal and systematic manner to share feedback, support, and critique is definitely something that students want (and deserve).

- Teachers will be more concerned with students liking them compared to teaching them.

  - The data say that per John Hattie's meta-analysis, teacher-student relationships matter more than second-chance programs like reading recovery, effective questioning strategies, and even small group learning.
  - What does that really mean? It is extremely difficult to find anything in this world involving humans where relationships do not matter. A direct lever to force teachers to treat students differently and possibly better is not something to cause concern. Quite simply, it is very difficult to learn from someone you do not like.

- Schools will be forced to keep less effective teachers.

  - The data say that the MET Project (2010) noted that the average student knows and understands what effective teaching is when he or she experiences it.
  - What does that really mean? The student who experiences someone's class for 170+ consecutive days probably has a decent grasp over who does his or her job well and who does not. The fear is that "easy" teachers will be the ones who are rated highly because they are liked and rigorous teachers will fall victim to harsh student critique. Previous analyses show this simply not to be the case.

- This is a frivolous, progressive idea that will never gain national traction. Let's wait it out.

  - The data say that Alaska implemented this in the 1990s.

- In 2012, the U.S. Department of Education launched the RESPECT project calling for teacher evaluations to be based on multiple perspectives and stakeholders. In 2010, the Gates Foundation called for similar processes.
- What does that really mean? The idea is not new and not without merit. The issue is that it simply has not become trendy yet in schools because fear has out influenced progress and common sense.

- This will create a toxic environment in the school.

  - The data say that Harvard Graduate School noted in a Project Zero study discussed by Brenda Burr at NAESP 2014 that the receptivity of student input was largely dependent on a safe and positive environment for students and adults (2014).
  - What does that really mean? For this to work, both students and adults must understand the rationale for this effort and see true purpose. This is the job of the leaders of the building—both formal and informal.

ELEVATING STUDENT VOICE—MAKING IT INVALUABLE

It Can Be Done, It Is Being Done

The seminal study regarding student participation in teacher evaluation began in 2009 under the guidance of Bill and Melinda Gates. The project studied over 3,000 teachers and was titled the Measures of Effective Teaching (MET). The study produced tremendous findings but universally noted that schools largely ignored student voice most commonly on high stakes issues. In essence, the more critical the issue, the less voice the students are given. This finding, while based out of study on student input on teacher evaluation in the smaller context, is truly why this book is so necessary. School leaders need to embrace the undeniable wisdom, brilliance, and creativity of our number one boss—the students.

The MET project noted four key findings necessary in order to guarantee student feedback to be both meaningful and useful.

- Measure what matters (PLAN).

  - This is a local decision and should be made as such.
  - Define expectations for both students and teachers.

- Have tools and resources to ensure accurate results (DO).
- Develop protocols to deliver the most accurate possible results (STUDY).

- Improvement of instruction and linkage to overall school improvement and student achievement goals should be present (ACT).

In essence, the study found that a continuous improvement cycle such as PDSA needs to be in place to make the best use of the information gathered.

Boston

Boston is a great poster child for listening to student voice, weathering the potential blowback, and moving forward collaboratively to create an even better product. Student leaders came together in 2006 and pushed for a voice in teacher evaluations. After a large amount of work, a comprehensive survey was developed and the program began to be rolled out.

As some would expect, this faced heavy scrutiny and blowback from certain teachers and the union at large. This led to years of policy review; however, this involved consistent student voice and continually made progress. In 2011, a state task force moved forward calling for mandatory student feedback in teacher evaluations. Since that time, the implementation of student voice on teacher evaluations has still been a learning experience with "kinks" to work out regarding applications at different grade levels and lingering concerns.

One major finding from the earliest implementation has been resoundingly clear according to Boston Public Schools officials—this has not been used as an opportunity to be vindictive toward teachers. In fact, the surveys and feedback mechanisms have provided quite the opposite.

Anchorage

Anchorage, the largest district in Alaska with over 50,000 students, has a different history and a different methodology. Over two decades ago, lawmakers in Alaska passed legislation calling for an opportunity to be provided for students to be included in teacher evaluations. The process Anchorage uses is very passive and does not require participation. The survey is open for the vast majority of the year and can be completed in school or online at home. The focus and rationale are convenience and accessibility.

While principals are expected to use the survey in teacher assessment, they have found that it is a great gauge of climate and connectedness. Viewing it through this lens, the district has been able to tailor questions to meet the unique circumstances and characteristics of each grade level. As a result, school officials currently find that the survey is best used to give an assessment of total school climate than it is used to determine individual teacher effectiveness.

Pittsburgh

In 2012, Pennsylvania legislators passed a measure requiring student feedback to encompass 15 percent of the overall teacher evaluation rating. Pittsburgh was well ahead of the curve in piloting such measures. Pittsburgh schools actually identify the fact that teachers were concerned with the validity of infrequent classroom visits and academic growth measures as the determinants of their evaluation rating. Pittsburgh notes that the data collected thus far are useful and stable. While Pittsburgh did note that the data are valuable, complexities arise when assigning ratings and percentages to the feedback received.

TAKEAWAYS AND LESSONS LEARNED

We do not have this right yet. There does not seem to be a systematic approach that has been deployed, learned from, improved upon, and set as the standard for using student feedback and voice on teacher evaluations. However, this is also not impossible. People are doing something. Students are not being vengeful and arbitrary. Some bargaining units have worked collaboratively to make this best work.

In fact, early returns are quite encouraging. People who have implemented this under a variety of conditions and circumstances seem to find that student feedback provides, at the very least, reliable data. In fact, a research synopsis published by Hanover Research (2013) found that the only greater predictor of student achievement gains than student feedback on teacher effectiveness was previous test score gains. Wow!

Additionally, given the intensity and scrutiny, a topic such as teacher evaluation brings forth some common decisions being made by districts wishing to give students a voice may seem a bit hypocritical. In order to ensure the best possible validity of surveys, many districts are using "canned" surveys such as The Tripod Survey or My Student Survey. The hypocrisy lies in wanting student voice to help inform teacher evaluation but not allowing student voice to exist in the creation of the instrument to be used.

To synthesize, we believe the following can be asserted and supported:

- Allowing students to have a voice on the performance of teachers when they are the one entity around the teacher most often simply makes common sense.
- Some states have moved toward (minimally) applying pressure to districts to consider this.
- Student perception surveys are being used with differing methodologies and intent in different districts.

- Student feedback is accurate, reliable, and overwhelmingly positive and professional.

Areas without research consensus or an exemplar model to follow:

- What survey instrument to use and how to arrive there?
- How often or when the evaluation instrument should be given?
- Should the surveys look different depending on the age of the students and/ or should surveys only begin at a set age?
- Should the feedback influence the teacher's evaluation rating or just be used for informational and growth planning purposes?
- Should this be mandatory or voluntary (for both students and teachers)?

NEXT STEPS

Throughout the entirety of this book, the acronym, ASK'EM, has been employed as a framework or methodology to use in order to best engage your students in a process and leverage their unique voice. This chapter is no different.

STAGE ONE: Exploring and Creating a System

ASK'EM

Ask: We need to understand whether or not students feel that there is a need for their input. Keeping students out of evaluation process has been such a long-standing tradition that students often have no idea this is even a possibility. They cannot conceptualize that they have been kept without a voice without someone directly asking.

Support: This is one area where students may not have a solution in mind when presented with this challenge. They will need support in finding resources, learning from others, and critically thinking to establish the best use of their voice.

Know: The thought of adding student voice to teacher evaluation is easy to imagine as stressful. When we think of the stress, however, we almost immediately think of the teacher. In speaking with students, this is also a stressful process for them. They will need to feel supported and protected throughout this new process as well.

Empower: Keep students a part of every element of this decision-making process. There is no part of this where their voice should not be heard. This underscores that this process must be collaborative at every turn. There is no way this works out well if teachers, administrators, and students are not a part of every aspect of this. All parties must find meaning, purpose, and benefit from engaging in this adaptive change.

Monitor: There are two key components to monitor as this dialogue begins. First, is the process moving forward? Anything that requires this much collaboration and consensus building has the tendency to bog down. It is important to keep moving forward. Second, is everyone involved at a level of comfortable discomfort? If people go from being comfortably uncomfortable to truly uncomfortable, their ability to progress ceases. We cannot let that occur.

STAGE TWO: Progressing through a Pilot

Ask—There must be a firm recognition that the intent of implementing student voice on teacher evaluation is not to simply say that we did so. The intent is to give students a mechanism to provide feedback that allows teachers and schools improve their practice. So it is important to continually ask students if they feel like they are being heard, but it is also essential to ensure that they are seeing evidence that the feedback they are providing is not falling on deaf ears. Remember—everyone wants feedback until something negative is said about him or her.

Support—Things will inevitably go wrong through this process. Supporting students and keeping their voice elevated are essential. Students need us to be their ally and their advocate. Support mechanisms may be as easy as sending students somewhere else to see a site visit to troubleshoot an implementation glitch or as complex as helping the students and the bargaining unit get on the same page.

Know—There is nothing more essential to having a great school than creating an environment where both adults and students feel safe and comfortable. Keeping a pulse on this during such a (potentially) combustible initiative is key. In fact, this may be the primary role that a school leader or lead student advocate plays in this process.

Empower—Students will see the glitches in the system. They will see the teachers that bristle the day after data are shared with them. They will see the percentage of students who do not take it seriously. They will see the small minority of kids who use this as an opportunity to lash out at teachers. We must empower them through this process to never stop speaking their truth and to never stop improving this process.

Monitor—As with any implementation, there must be some measure of success for which you can monitor progress against. This initiative is widely ranging that it can be anything from culture and climate surveys (we would encourage examining HUMANeX Ventures survey platforms) to tracking student engagement or achievement. This is the key piece, however. We must teach our students that doing something for the sake of doing something is not good enough. Establishing this culture allows for students to also "own" the monitoring phase of implementation.

A QUICK NOTE TO TEACHERS READING THIS BOOK

Student voice as part of performance evaluation is potentially invaluable. Their voice is authentic, and their experiences have been true and rich. We encourage you to lead a movement to this end in our nation's schools (and across the world), but even without schoolwide support, one can implement this in their own classroom. In fact, doing so and showing systemwide excitement to learn about what we all can do better will have a dramaticly positive impact on all students.

Teacher evaluation has become a primary focus of reform efforts in schools, yet we have created systems that allow our students to be rendered mute in this process. We believe that when you have the will to provide practitioners clear and concise suggestions on how to give students the opportunity to provide input on this time-intensive, stressful, and meaningful process, significant improvement will occur.

SUMMARY

We do not believe any of us reading this book would design a system where the people with the most direct contact with someone would have no input on that person's performance assessment.

There is no commonsense reason why schools do not ask students for feedback on teacher performance during the performance evaluation process. There have been many excuses made about why this cannot or should not happen.

This chapter debunks all of these excuses with research and data-based evidence that everyone's biggest fears will *not* become a reality. A school cannot truly proclaim that it provides an avenue to student voice and then not include our number one customer during the evaluation process. In this chapter, we provided guidance on how to change both mind-sets and behaviors.

Conclusion

One of the greatest phrases in education is "the smartest person in the room *is* the room." This, or something of similar meaning, is said frequently during professional development, committee work, or other times designated and delineated for collaboration. One of the biggest issues facing our schools today, and something truly holding schools back from radical and transformational change, is that this mentality is rarely employed when it comes to working with students.

We have observed that many leaders in our industry fail to exhibit the belief that students have brilliance when it comes to the struggles and challenges facing schools, regardless of us championing their potential and capacity in myriad other areas. This disconnect must stop. If this book does anything for you as the reader, the hope is that you take a moment to pause and think about major decisions, traditions, items accepted as the status quo, and rules and change that are under your control. Ask yourself if you consulted students in any significant manner on each item.

Experience indicates that in most schools, students are kept out of most decisions and there is *no* good reason why. There is a plethora of excuses being made, but none of them stand up. Simply put, no other industry systematically ignores the voice of the customer as much as education.

A great photo gets shared often on Twitter, with people encouraging principals to hang it on their office door. The picture is of a caution sign that reads, "Warning, your principal is about to ask you if this is what is best for kids." This kids-first mentality is great. However, as educators and leaders, we often impart our wisdom on what is best for kids without ever consulting them.

This book is about one thing—building upon the kids-first mentality that all great educators have and transforming the mentality of serving kids first to serving *with* kids first. This book is our call to action. This book should provide a sense of urgency and a corresponding hope for the future. Our greatest asset is (and always will be) our students.

For schools, which are notoriously slow to adopt change, to stay current in our exponentially changing world we must listen to the kids we serve. They are our greatest link to the future, which schools often say they are preparing them for. If we want to transform our schools to look like the real world and to look like the environment kids thrive in, we must stop and listen.

In reading this book, you have been called on to evaluate a subset of practices in your school and you have been given guidance on how to transform these practices into ones that incorporate student voice and challenge the status quo of adult-driven decision making in your buildings. To review, the topics and the primary challenges issued and guidance provided were as follows:

Decision Making—This chapter explores the big rock of "decision making." As teachers and leaders, we do a decent job of including student voice on trivial matters but keep them far away from the truly impactful decisions. We explore that trend and provide guidance on how to effectively move forward.

Building Our Community of Learners—Schools often talk about how they want to prepare students to be productive members of the community but refuse to allow the time necessary to do so or allow students to truly explore what is important to them. This book explores easy ways to increase student voice in what many schools identify as their mission.

Digital Citizenship—Digital citizenship is a necessary skill for today's students to have that is too often ignored. We explore how to include student voice and opinion in what our students need to safely and productively live in the digital age.

1:1 Initiatives—Guidance is provided on how to ensure that our technology initiatives are really learning initiatives by incorporating student voice.

School Design and Structures—It is fairly easy to tell what decade a school was built in when you walk in based on the architecture du jour. The new age of schooling calls for flexible seating and changing environments, if not entirely new classrooms or buildings. In this process, most schools are assuming the most recent article they have read or design their architect shows them is what is best for kids. However, too many times we are not asking students what they want and need in order to be successful.

District Communication and Branding—School branding was once something only on the radar of very few teachers and school leaders. Now, it has become part of the job. This chapter discusses how this "other duty as assigned" through the evolution of education can and should be shared with our students. If our number one customer cannot tell a positive story about our schools, then there are more issues than poor PR that need to be addressed.

Personalized Learning—Is there anything in any way that can be truly personalized without consult of the person the material is being individualized for? We explore how to better incorporate student voice in personalized learning, the curricular base of the future.

Equity in Education—Teachers, school staff, and school leaders often champion the causes of those traditionally underserved in education. However, leveraging student voice allows schools to present an entirely different and more compelling argument to create systemic change and provide equity in education.

Teacher Evaluation—Somehow, it has become the norm in schools to deny those with the most access to teachers any voice in their performance assessment. Research and innovative districts have worked to disprove many of the negative assumptions that accompany any suggestion of this type. This book provides helpful hints and encouragement on how to effectively utilize student voice in order to best support the growth of our teachers.

ASK'EM AND STOP, THINK, ACT

Throughout the entirety of this work, we have used the acronym, ASK'EM, and the process of Stop, Think, Act to walk readers through each of our main ideas. In closing, we will do so one last time.

Stop: Continuing to introduce, legislate, and enforce change or reinforce the status quo without engaging in meaningful dialogue with our students.

Think: If we are attempting to create the leaders of our world tomorrow, why would we not engage them in the leadership of our schools today?

Act: Start today and work to create systems to ensure that you connect meaningfully with students about all major aspects of school life. To begin, use the ASK'EM model!

ASK'EM

Ask: Ask students to think big, and ask them to think about where their voice being heard would have the greatest impact on the school.

Support: We have taken some of the brilliance from students over time, and they may not know how to react to this question. It is your job to ensure that they reach into their kindergarten heart and mind to be fearless and to guarantee that their imagination has no bounds.

Know: Nobody knows your kids as well as you do. This is a change, and it is a change that they may not initially trust. It is going to most likely take leadership at the individual student level to help create student ownership as part of the culture of your building.

Empower: Great leaders set floors for performance, but never ceilings. Create an environment that empowers your students to lead change and dream big.

Monitor: Giving students an opportunity to have their voice heard and not acting on it will cause significant regression in your building. It is important to understand that this process is fluid and ongoing. Change is incremental and not linear. It is necessary to monitor the level of success of incorporating student voice at every turn.

One of the book's central questions was why should today's school leaders engage student voice from a leadership perspective as collaborators in leading? Another was how can today's school leaders engage student voice from a leadership perspective as collaborator in leading? Now you are ready to do all you can to elevate student voice from invisible to invaluable! We charge you with the responsibility and support to *ASK'EM!*

References

Brown, J. L., Domenech, D., & Sherman, M. (2016). *Personalizing 21st century education*. San Francisco, CA: Jossey-Bass.

Bullis, B., Filippi, J., & Lubelfeld, M. (2016). Reimagined NGSS learning spaces: Principals as holistic school improvement leaders. *Principal Leadership*, 52–54 May/June 2017.

Burr, B. (2014). Student voice in teacher evaluations. Presentation slides for NAESP. Retrieved from https://www.naesp.org/sites/default/files/images/as/StudentVoice_in_Teacher_handout1.pdf

Duran, L., & Herold, B. (2016, May 17). 1-to-1 laptop initiatives boost student scores, study finds first-of-its-kind analysis examines 15 years of data. *Education Week*. *35,* 8–11.

Education Reimagined. (2015). A transformational vision for education in the US. Washington, DC: Convergence.

Hanover Research. (2013). Student perception surveys and teacher assessments: Prepared for XYZ. Retrieved from https://dese.mo.gov/sites/default/files/Hanover-Research-Student-Surveys.pdf

Kouzes, J. M., & Posner, B. Z. (2007). *The leadership challenge*. San Francisco, CA: Jossey-Bass.

Lubelfeld, M., & Polyak, N. (2016). How school superintendents explored future learning together [Keyword blog: Google Education.] Retrieved from https://www.blog.google/topics/education/how-school-superintendents-explored-future-learning-together/

Lubelfeld, M., & Polyak, N. (2017). *The unlearning leader: Leading for tomorrow's schools today*. Lanham, MD: Rowman & Littlefield.

Marcinek, A. (2015). *The 1 to 1 roadmap: Setting the course for innovation in education*. Thousand Oaks, CA: Corwin.

Marzano, R., & Waters, T. (2005). *School leadership that works: From research to results*. Alexandria, VA: Association for Supervision and Curriculum Development.

MET Project. (2010). Learning about teaching: Initial findings from the measures of effective teaching project. Bill and Melinda Gates Foundation. www.metproject.org.

MET Project. (2012). Asking students about teaching: Student perception surveys and their implementation. Bill and Melinda Gates Foundation. www.metproject.org.

Murray, T., & Sheninger, E. (2017). *Learning transformed: 8 keys to designing tomorrow's schools today*. Alexandria, VA: Association for Supervision and Curriculum Development.

Nevins A., & Commager H.S. (1992). A Pocket History of the United Stated. New York: Simon & Schuster).

Quaglia et al. (2016). School voice report 2016. Quaglia Institute for School Voice and Aspirations and Corwin Press.

About the Authors

Phillip J. "PJ" Caposey, Ed.D.
P. J. Caposey is an award-winning educator leading his small rural school to multiple national recognitions as a principal and has done the same as a superintendent. PJ is an active member of the greater educational community voicing opinions and providing training and consult on many topics. PJ is the author of three books and is a sought-after speaker and consultant specializing in school culture, principal coaching, effective evaluation practices, and student-centered instruction. Recently, PJ has been named a NSPRA Superintendent to Watch, 40 Leaders Under 40 honoree, and Eastern Illinois University's Distinguished Educator Award winner. PJ currently serves as the superintendent of schools for Meridian CUSD 223 in northwest Illinois and is married to his wife, Jacquie, and has four children. PJ can be reached via twitter @MCUSDSupe.

Michael Lubelfeld, Ed.D.
Mike currently serves as the superintendent of schools in the Deerfield Public Schools (District 109), Illinois. Mike earned his doctor of education in curriculum and instruction from Loyola University of Chicago, where his published dissertation was on *Effective Instruction in Middle School Social Studies*. He is also on the adjunct faculty at National Louis University in the Department of Educational Leadership. Mike has earned an IASA School of Advanced Leadership Fellowship, and he has also graduated from the AASA National Superintendent Certification Program. He can be found on Twitter at @mikelubelfeld, and he is the co-moderator of #suptchat—the superintendent educational chat on Twitter. He and Nick Polyak authored the 2017 Rowman & Littlefield book *The Unlearning Leader: Leading for*

Tomorrow's Schools Today. Mike has been married to his wife, Stephanie, for the past fourteen years, and they have two children.

Nick Polyak, Ed.D.

Dr. Polyak is the proud superintendent of the award-winning Leyden Community High School District 212. He earned his undergraduate degree from Augustana College in Rock Island, Illinois, his master's from Governors State University, and his Ed.D. from Loyola University Chicago. Nick has been a classroom teacher and coach, a building and district-level administrator, a school board member, and a superintendent for the past eight years in both central Illinois and suburban Chicago. Nick has earned an IASA School of Advanced Leadership Fellowship, and he also graduated from the AASA National Superintendent Certification Program. He can be found on Twitter at @npolyak, and he is the co-moderator of #suptchat—the superintendent educational chat on Twitter. Nick has been married to his wife, Kate, for the past seventeen years, and they have four children.

HOW DO YOU LEARN BEST?

Take your free survey at
studentvoice.humanexventures.com

Introducing the HUMANeX Ventures
Sensory Preference Inventory™

Continued learning and development starts at the foundation – first understanding HOW you learn best. Having a clear understanding if you are a VISUAL, AUDITORY, or KINESTHETIC learner can greatly impact the way in wich you learn and grow in your life and career.

Three Reasons Learning Styles are Important

1. Ensure information is received most effectively for long-term learning and growth.
2. Keep yourself engaged and learning for longer periods of time.
3. Use time more effectively in your learning and how you teach others.

 & **#suptchat** In partnership with **HUMANeX** VENTURES ✖